THE PLAYER

How I Discovered the Dark Side of the Game

Part 2

Bostjan Belingar

NEW Foreword by RSD Max

Copyright

The Player: How I Discovered the Dark Side of the Game, Part 2, by Bostjan Belingar

1st edition

www.bosslifehacks.com

For permissions, general inquiries, or just to say hello, use the email address below:

bostjan.belingar@gmail.com

ISBN: 978-961-283-952-9

Foreword by Maximilian Berger (RSD Max)
Cover Pic by Fabien Normand: www.fabiennormand.ch
Editing by Josiah Davis Book Services:
www.jdbookservices.com
Writing Support by Now Novel:
www.nownovel.com

Disclaimer:

I have tried to recreate events, locales, and conversations from my memories of them. In order to maintain their anonymity in some instances I have altered the names of individuals and places, I may have changed some identifying characteristics and details such as physical properties, occupations, and places of residence.

Dedication

This book is dedicated to any guy who has ever battled with the fear of talking to a girl they fancied. It's a long and difficult journey, but it's well worth it. Persist.

Dear Seb

Here's the 2ⁿᵈ, slightly darker part of the adventures. It's kinnda like in life - it sucks when it's happening, but ultimately teaches you more. Hope it inspires you for adventures of your own!

Bostjan

RSD MAX ♡

barcelona, 17th Jan 2018

Table Of Contents

For Pirates

Look, I used to pirate a lot. Music, books, films, games, software, you name it.

I'm doing it less now, mainly for two reasons. Number one, there is a lot of free, quality content on the web. Number two, I'm not broke anymore, I have some money, and if a piece of work moves me, or teaches me a valuable lesson, I don't mind paying the price.

So if you are reading this book and didn't buy it, I understand. However, if the book speaks to you, resonates with you, or if it teaches you something, I ask you to do something for me.

If you're broke, drop me a note and let me know you enjoyed it. It means a lot. Share the book or one of my videos on social media, recommend me to someone.

If you do have some money, PayPal (shoot me an email for details) what you think the book is worth to me, or go buy one on Amazon. If you want, drop a note with it too, so I know where it's coming from.

And now enjoy the book. Arrr Arrr!

Foreword

When you truly love something, you let it kill you.

Sounds so romantic, so fascinating, like I'm the martyr of my own life. Go get a piece of me before I'm deflated, nothing but an empty shell.

Yeah… that sounds about right, then I'll be happy.

It sounds good on paper, it even feels good for a short while, but in reality it's a nightmare.

Hi, my name is Max and I'm a dating coach. I traveled the world 3 times to teach guys how to get laid, pursue their dreams, find their dream girl and live a happy life. Only thing is… I can't do it myself.

I'm dead inside, I can't talk, not even to my own family, I don't reply to texts of my girlfriends… dim shadows somewhere behind a thick layer of the mist that was once called my mind. I sleep 17h a day, I shove food in my face whenever I can, my eyes stare into the distance and I'm spending most of my waking hours watching people on Youtube play video games.

Yep, when you truly love something you let it kill you. So romantic.

Now don't worry, I'm good nowadays, I lead a happy life, surrounded by great people, I take time off, I travel less, I lift more, I feel better. But at the end of my 3 years of touring I couldn't have felt more like shit and to be honest I don't think I would have made it without Bostjan.

You see, I was stupid, in my early 20s (and I can say that now, literally just turned 27 a couple hours ago lol) and I literally thought I was invincible. I was busting out 17h work days with ease, no remorse, no thought about longevity, just full-on pedal-to-the-metal 7 days a week. Video recording, video editing, Free Tour speeches, Bootcamp 1:1 coaching, more video editing, Hot Seat seminars, more video editing, a quick pull of some hottie here and there... although that soon got replaced by more video editing. Bostjan was actually the first one who mentioned the concept of "one day off per week, please!" haha.

I loved it, I loved every second of it. Every single video cut, every word on my Youtube channel, every speech in front of a crowd, every girl I talked to, every Facebook post, every Instagram picture... it was all a tiny piece of me.

And little by little I gave those pieces away. I called it "expansion" but in reality it was "deflation". Giving away everything of yourself until you have nothing left FOR yourself. I truly didn't know who I was some 14 months into the tour. I was this empty shell of a "pickup artist", a laughable puppet of deep inner instincts. I need to fuck, eat, shit and coach. All day. For the rest of my life.

There IS a dark side to game. There is an even darker side if you teach it, because you can't just fuck off and take your favorite girl off to an exotic island until you feel refreshed again (hint: I did that after 3 years for the first time, works like a charm ;)), we were in the middle of another world tour, every week a new city, new faces, new challenges.

This book delves deep into a period of my life I will never fucking forget. It's actually even hard to write about it now. It was December 2015, Gothenburg, Sweden. The land of the beauties, I had money, my brand had huge momentum, the Max Hot Seat had just broken all records, people recognizing me on the street, airports, in the gym, and of course in the clubs. Game has become something automatic, robotic, easy. But I didn't care about all that. I had been dead for months. It must've been 4am in the morning, Bostjan and Vini both sleeping, but I couldn't. I couldn't for the last 3 months.

Insomnia. Depression. Burnout. Another fucking night of self-hate: "Max, you gotta get up in literally one hour and prepare the Hot Seat… and you still couldn't fall asleep, you loser…" I'm staring out the window, another 2000-calorie shake in my hand and that ONE THOUGHT popped into my head: "Hey what if I just jump out of the window and fly… it'll be all over just like that…"

Wow. I take a step back. That was scary. I was always a rather positive person, depression and sleep deprivation may come and go but I was never SUICIDAL. Granted, it was just that one thought, but still scary I gotta say.

You know, when you live to give you might end up giving too much. That was that.

Then there were girls. The reason everyone got into the game in the first place. Sure as hell most of us stay for the spiritual work, the self development, the motivation and inspiration. But we all get into it to get some pussy first, haha.

But it's tough after a while, it's tough if you go out to such a great degree that you find yourself talking to "yet another hottie" in some random country, she's talking about the EXACT SAME THINGS you've heard hundreds of girls talk about before. Funny enough the most frequent one you hear is: "I'm not like any other girl", hahaha. You know EXACTLY what she's gonna do next, you know EXACTLY what's going to happen at the end of the night and yes, to be fully honest it's kinda disappointing.

See, girls are beautiful, girls are a wonderful god-sent gift that descended down from heaven to make us men realize that we need to man the fuck up. Nobody's gonna wanna fuck a broke loser with no dreams. Man up, learn how to be yourself, work on yourself every day and boom happiness awaits you, women will be a side effect of that.

HOWEVER after having been on so many dates with girls who have a boyfriend, after fucking the shit out of married women, while their little husband is home with the kids... After having threesomes, after chick-sharing girls that feel the urgent need to announce "I'm not that kind of girl" while unzipping my friends pants while I fuck her from behind... After catching them lying over and over again... Well, it's kinda hard to ever fully trust a girl again.

Don't get me wrong, everyone lies, men lie, assholes lie, but girls... man... it hits you way harder. You grow up adoring pretty girls, you imagine a perfect character behind the beautiful face, you project a perfect life onto them. But well, reality is always different, isn't it?

Sex. Sex... that beautiful thing where two bodies melt into one, the climax of a fun date out with a gorgeous girl, the ultimate connection between two individuals. Meh. Once you get it over and over again, once you realize you can fuck as many hot blonde girls with b-cup tits, high heels and tight asses as you can, but STILL don't feel happy inside... it kinda loses its edge.

You ask if you can take pictures of them while they lie next to you in bed… so you can have some sort of "souvenir" for when you're back on the road again. Most of them love the idea and a week later all that's left is a grainy iPhone pic of some random hottie covered in bedsheets and jizz. You try to remember her story, her passions, her ambitions, for God's sake you try to remember HER NAME. Nothing. Still emptiness.

Fuck going out, fuck socializing, I need to have time for myself. People coming up to me "dude, thanks for everything, you changed my life!", well then why can't you leave me alone, then? Every hand shakes costs effort, every smile kills me inside, I can't.

I remember at some point I'm standing in the corner of a seminar room, I had just spoken for 10 straight hours, people are getting up to leave, they're pumped, they're hyped, most of them wanna come up to me and shake my hand. Bostjan is standing next to me, he's starting to pack the camera gear. I ask him to stay. Just stay next to me bro, please don't leave me alone with all these people. He always did, he always took care of everyone.

Like I said, if it hadn't been for Bostjan I think I wouldn't have made it lol, I might have ACTUALLY pissed off to some exotic island, throwing it all down the drain. He was always making sure (or at least trying to) that Vini and me got some time off, that we would go off watch some fucking movie or whatever. He always carried as much of the burden as possible.

Yeah, coaching life is tough, you stop trusting most girls, you stop going out at some point and then it comes. Freedom. August 2016, I have just launched the Natural, the program that is everything. The program that has so much of me I'm sure you could use the information in there to clone my ass and have me live on forever lol. The tour is over. I'm back in Austria. I'm at my mom's wedding, she's marrying a cool dude and everyone is happy. I brought Bostjan, he's socializing, people love him... and I'm standing in the corner dead out of my mind. It's my family but I'm still way too fucked up to really talk to anybody. You know, maybe that's why I invited Bostjan to the wedding… maybe I subconsciously knew I wouldn't make it through without him lol.

This book describes the slow descent of three dudes on tour. They're traveling the world, yet they're isolated. It's only them. People come and go, girls come and go, but at the end of the day it's only them. Another seminar room, another airplane ride, another fucking hotel room. Only them.

This book is about game, this book is about the dark side of game. This book is about the hustle. This book is about adventure, growth and dead passions. But at the end of the day this book is about friendship.

Enjoy,

RSD Max

Chapter One

YOU CAN SLEEP ANYWHERE – IF TIRED ENOUGH

Tallinn, December 2015

From Eastern Europe, our next stop was the North. The first city: Tallinn, Estonia. And it's a kind of awesome symbolism as well. The year had turned from autumn to winter, from the bright and final colors of gold to dark and gloomy. And my journey went from "omg this traveling and chasing pussy is so cool," to some more mature and, later on, dark, realizations.

Tallinn is far from my favorite city. It's small, cold, you can't really go out. The girls didn't seem too hot. It's also not very cheap, at least the food. The only thing it has going for it is it's beautiful medieval city centre. There was a gorgeous castle with a big wall and large towers. I guess it was epic for shooting historical movies.

We had a very late flight that day. I think we landed around 11pm. Most of the shops in that little airport were closed and we were dead tired. Still, the hustle rolls on if you want it or not. Max grabbed SIM cards for himself and Vini, so we could Uber to Max's Airbnb. I would be staying with the crew this time.

I tried finding a host in the Tallinn FB Inner Circle, but couldn't. It's a pretty small group and it doesn't seem too active - I think it was the first time that nobody offered a couch. I was pretty stressed out – cash was slowly running out, and I would have to get some hostel for the week. But then Max surprised me and said:

"Relax, bro. You can stay with us, we'll smuggle you in."

The Airbnb was only booked for two, so I would be there illegally, which means Max would get into trouble if someone found me there.

As Max is getting an Uber for us, I notice Vini lying on the floor. He was legit lying on the floor, in his coat, with shades on. Vini can goof around a lot, he's got a sort of sly and intelligent humor going on, very sarcastic a lot of the time. But I think that time he was just really fucking tired.

Uber brings us to the place, and I jump out of the car and go try to find some coffee place that's still open. As Max and Vini were meeting the Airbnb host and discussing the flat conditions, I had to be somewhere else. It was only supposed to be 2 guys in the flat.

Unlucky for me, there was no open places around me, and I couldn't care to walk around too much. Remember, I was fully loaded, my big blue suitcase and a full backpack. So I just zipped my jacket all the way up, put on my hat and waited. It was cold and wet, so it was a very shitty wait.

"Hey bro, you can come now, the host left. The door code is 1572, we're in the 2nd floor. You'll see. Catch you soon."

I come inside, happy for the warmth and notice that there's no couch in the common area. Max and Vini have rooms of their own and all that remains is the good old floor.

At this point I was so tired I didn't give a shit anymore. The guys gave me some extra blankets they didn't need and I fished for some extra pillows, and then created a sort of bed on the floor.

It was pretty uncomfortable, but I still slept like a baby.

If you can't sleep, you might just not be tired enough.

Chapter Two
A MILF HANDJOB

HJ Report, Tallinn Inner Circle Facebook Group

I wasn't sure if I would go out or not, Max and Vini stayed in this time.

I took a power nap at 11pm and… fell asleep. Woke up at 2am, did some work, and then finally decided just to take a look around, left the house at 2.30am. Yes, I was very horny. Going solo at first felt a bit awkward, but then I pushed those thoughts away and surrendered to my inner pimp, which always knows what to do.

Nice.

So I hit the first pub, Tallinn is super fucking dead, there were almost ZERO people out. Keep in mind, this is Estonia's capital city, what the fuck. There was a total amount of ten people in the first 2 bars I found. And none of them could tell me where I could get some weed either. Not the best impression of Tallinn so far.

Third place was finally a bit better, about 20-30 people in total, mostly mixed sets. I see an older girl sitting alone, EASY!

I chat with her for a bit, she's into me. Some dude comes and smiles at her, first I ignore him, then I think that he might be a friend, so I acknowledge him and smile:

"Yo, hey man."

I suspect he might be a player himself (but later change my mind because he sucked so badly) and wants to steal the girl. So I just fully ignore him. It's funny how people don't know how to deal with being ignored. He gets mad and says he will kick me but I just keep ignoring and move his hand away when he tries to tap my shoulder:

"No violence bro, no violence."

After some time I screen her for spontaneity. She's into drugs, she won't work the next day. Great, that means if we both like each other, she will probably be down to have sex. I bounce her to the other room, which has a ping pong table and a DJ. Random thought, why would you have a DJ and a ping pong table in the same room?

The girl and I sit down, chat, and she's super physical on me. So quite soon we make out, but then I quickly break:

"No we can't, I don't know you well enough."

She gives me a funny laugh and a look that could be saying: "Bitch please, I'm too old for this shit."

By the way, she's 36 and not very hot, I guess okay looking for 36. Short, slightly chubby, dark hair, a regular face, not the best sense of style. She also smells of cigarettes. Yes, I know. I did say I was super horny, don't judge...

I bounce her to the corridor, we make out a bit more, I try to pull already, but she doesn't wanna come, so I just leave her. I go back in, open a mixed three-set with two chicks and play around a bit. They love me, but have to leave soon. I go into the main area, open another three-set with one girl from before, they open well but they're not really DTF (down to fuck).

#Down-To-Fuck (DTF)
How much a girl is in a state of mind to have sex that night.

Here's the thing about DTF. Girls are like guys, they get horny regularly. I mean, it's normal, we as a species have sex on the list of basic needs. It's not bad or "dirty", just check Maslow's hierarchy, sex is next to food. It's not at the top with contribution needs, it's next to food and water.

So basically, a percentage of girls in a club will be very similar to us guys, super horny and down to fuck somebody that night. Sometimes, and again speaking for both genders, the person who we want to have sex with is not narrowly defined. We just want to have sex with someone that's within our standards.

More or less cute, more or less charming, with more or less of a connection. These standards can rise or drop proportionally to the amount of alcohol we do or don't consume. But the point is, sex is a basic need, and a percentage of both genders in the club will just be down to fuck that night.

However, there's one thing fundamentally different for girls here. It's much more socially unacceptable for a girl to just fuck someone she met that night. She will be called a slut, and "easy." Whereas a guy who has sex with a lot of girls is approved of as a player. I hate double standards.

Anyway, I had already opened most girls by this time. Then I see the milf with the guy from before and go join them for a bit. Just for a bit of fun.

I just say "Hi," sit next to them and do nothing, as I see the guy is a drunk chode. So she naturally starts to be interested in me again, without me doing anything but sitting there. Well, she did see me hitting on all other chicks too. I give her a bit of attention, she likes me, but still talks to the guy too though. I don't mind, I just check my phone from time to time and chill.

At some point the guy goes for a smoke, so I chat with her, talk about drugs and after that about anal sex because that's what we both like. At this point in the travel, hardly anything could surprise me. I get the logistics. I try to pull again at this stage, but she doesn't wanna come. Fine, more chilling then.

The guy comes back but is still a drunk chode, bad luck for you, bro. I sense her looking to me from time to time. I re-engage, the guy just disappears at some point. She becomes physical again, I bounce her to the ping pong room, then to the corridor again, we make out. Heavy make out, she's super turned on, I touch and squeeze the sides of her torso (rib area, super erotic), later go for her ass.

She touches my dick and grasps my intense boner. I did say I was really horny didn't I? I whisper in her ears:

"Yeah, you feel how hard I am for you baby. Yeah, you wanna touch my hard cock, baby. Yeah, you probably wanna suck my dick baby, huh..."

She's moaning like crazy and dry humping my leg at this point. She starts putting hands in my pants and boxers and rubbing my hard dick but I'm like:

"No, we can't here. Let's go."

I try to pull her out, but again, she won't come with me. Then I try to pull to the toilet, but I don't know where it is, I'm such a fucking retard.

I tell her:

"Show me the toilet baby."

She won't. Oh, boy, this is becoming complicated, haha. I ask her a few minutes later, while making out again:

"Do you want me to fuck you tonight?"

"Yes!"

But when I try to pull again she won't. Then at some point I leave her, go downstairs, and finally I find the toilet.

Dynamics changed though. She's evading me now. I'm becoming slightly desperate. I go out, to see if she will follow. She doesn't. When I go in I see her again, I try to lead her to the toilet, but she's not interested. I can't be bothered anymore, she's not even hot.

Quite frustrated, I return back home at 5am, jerk off, eat, and then it's bedtime. When I am drifting to sleep, the image of the old girl appears in my mind, transformed and grotesque. I start to wonder what made me so horny and what made me chase a girl that didn't really attract me, neither physically nor emotionally.

The confusion is thankfully dispelled by the blissful sleep.

Chapter Three
DARKNESS & GYM

The atmosphere in Tallinn was incredibly grim. We worked even harder than usual, so our biorhythms got even worse. We would go to bed at 4am and wake up around 12 or 1pm. By the time we were ready to leave the house for gym, filming or other errands, the sun would be gone and it would be pitch black already. We actually didn't get to see the sun for the whole week there.

We went out one day to shoot videos and take some pictures for Instagram. Also, as a note here, us doing Instagram pictures for Max is different than just taking some pics with your friends. This was business. You see, traveling also had a role of portraying the lifestyle, and a traveling lifestyle is what draws in a lot of people.

So we'd make sure we took some really sick pictures of Max (and ourselves too, because why not) in every city. Good poses, good light, always next to some landmarks. Then Max would send those to his team and they'd tweak the colors, add some motivational quotes or captions and send them back. The result were those inspirational and motivational pictures that you can see if you scroll through your social media news feed.

I remember one picture of Max under the castle. I held the light as Vini was taking the pic. It was a really good pic, yet Max's face seemed a little paler than usual when I looked at the pic later. I took no heed of it then, but remembered it somewhat later.

Even my memories of Tallinn are not really vivid. I mostly remember hitting the gym. It was a really nice gym, five minutes from our Airbnb, and Max paid our weekly passes for the gym so we hit it almost every day. We didn't have all the regular events in Tallinn, only the Bootcamp, which gave us a lot of free time.

I also remember working a lot. And I remember a certain frustrating girl I talked to and hung out with after a Bootcamp night. But as said, my memories of Tallinn are not so vivid, maybe it has something to do with the whole darkness thing, I don't know. I also recall Tallinn as being the highest frustration point for me as a player. But I'll get to that a little later.

I noticed Max sleeping a lot. Like, a lot. So if we'd all go to bed at like 4am or 5am, he would sometimes sleep until 2pm or 3pm, about 11 hours. It was not normal for him, but he seemed fine otherwise. He would still hit the gym regularly and he'd do all the work, so everything seemed fine, though a bit unusual. Later on I realized he even mentioned some peculiar things himself:

"Dude, we're literally missing all the sunlight. Check it out, I woke up at 2pm today, and as we were hitting the gym at around 4, the sun was already gone, it was dark outside. I feel like I'm in a video game, haha."

He said that with a smile on his face, and with a "check how cool this is" voice, but it seemed a bit off. I even told him that I don't mind some sun and don't like the fact that it gets dark so fast.

The signs of wear and tear started to show on the whole crew, me included, despite being on the road for the least time. After two months of hardcore travel and work (and all else included), I was getting seriously tired. I'd finish pimping a little earlier. I'd sleep a little more. I'd eat a little less healthy.

The guys had it way worse. Vini had been on tour at that point for about 10 months already. 10 months of traveling, clubbing 3-5 days every week, video editing, shooting vids, eating cheap food, and changing the country every week.

And Max had been doing that for nearly two years as an instructor, and half a year before that for his own assistantship. I can't even imagine how it was for him. Two years on the road, no home, city to city, girl to girl.

I only understood the scope of it later, when he said things like:

"Dude, you and Vini are literally the only people I know. Sometimes I wake up, and I have no idea where I am. It's really confusing at some points. Another random city, with random people, random students. You guys are the only constant..."

We had a super interesting talk with Max and Vini too. Very personal.

We filmed it for one of Max's video blogs, but it was set up as a personal conversation between the three of us. And the topic discussed was why us guys, players especially, so many times try to get together with girls who are "broken."

By broken I mean the little shy girls, who believe they are not good enough. The girls who probably had it bad when growing up, and still feel incapable of love, or feel worthless, or ugly, despite the reality being obviously different. And the funny thing was a part of us players just wanted to be the white knight in the shining armor, to save the little broken girls and show them the nice world outside.

#White Knight

A guy who sees the typical maiden in distress and believes that he can help her. He sees the girl as the pure innocent goddess, who cannot help or save herself. Here his chivalry and virtue shine, and he charges to the rescue.

I am over-simplifying a lot here, but this is not how it works. It's quite foolish to think that the girl cannot save herself, in fact, it's quite derogatory. Only one person can ever change somebody, and that person is the person themselves. There is no other way, even though we all wish differently at some point.

There were a few highlights in the week too. During the day game Bootcamp on Sunday, Vini agreed to eat a whole 1kg jar of Jelly Beans for 10€. Max loved to make bets like that.

"Yo, Vini, bro, I'll give you 10€ if you eat the whole Jelly Bean pack."

Vini, liking easy money, happily agreed. I was just thinking about the amount of sugar in that jar and threw up in my mind. I don't think I'd eat that for $100. In the end, he couldn't even eat half, and he became somewhat sick from all the sugar. He seemed to feel ill, so I didn't rub it in his face too much.

The next highlight, and something Vini would later on give as a preparation speech for Max's Free Tour talk in Sweden, was a crazy gym story.

The whole crew was in the gym, working out. Max was on his phone as usual, texting and dropping voice messages to girls in between the sets. At some point, he just disappears. Vini and I didn't even notice, because we were making a photo shooting session in the gym after working out. Gotta show that 6-pack, right?

About an hour later, Max returns and updates me and Vini.

"Remember that funny Tinder girl I've been texting and trolling with today? So yeah, I just went to see her, we fucked, and now I'm back to finish the leg set."

That was somewhat hilarious and somewhat inspirational, Vini and I were blown away. I've seen a lot lately, but Max still surprised me regularly, either with his game, or his hustling ethic. Or his increasingly dark mood.

But all in all, most of the things I remember from Tallinn was a lot of darkness, the gym, and the massive frustration regarding the girls.

Let me explain.

Chapter Four
TWO DAYGAME
PULLS AT WORK

Field Report, Tallinn Inner Circle Facebook Group

So it's a Sunday afternoon and, as usual, I'm working. A day game Bootcamp.

Filming in some shopping mall, making some jokes with the crew. At some point I say, quite loudly as usual (we really didn't give much of a crap what anyone would thought of us):

"Aw, I have some much shit in my pants that they will literally fall off." And some girl from a shop nearby hears me and laughs: "I hope they don't." I pop into the shop.

I know I have to close her fast, cause I have to film. So I just bullshit a little, call her out on her checking my pecs out, introduce myself, and make plans for coffee later. I take her number down and then proceed to text with her as I work. It was about 6pm.

Then we hit another shopping mall, we're about to finish the Bootcamp at 8.00, it's 7.30pm now and I have a plan to meet the chick from before at 9pm for coffee, after she closes her shop. During the Bootcamp brief, we see a smoking hot blonde. Awesome style, slender, long, straight blonde hair, beautiful face. A perfect girl, at least from the distance.

Max points her out and calls me out to open her. You see, what good friends and wings that know you well will do is push you. They'll dare you to seduce some girl, usually in a situation where you would not act on your own. Expanding the comfort zone for you with the tool of pressure.

I'm like "Damn man, really...", but just start moving my legs and end up going there anyway. It's just another girl. Some food promoter talks to her just before I do, so I just wait a bit and then open her myself. She opens well and we have a conversation.

With this girl I gamed a bit more on point than usual. In retrospect, I discovered a major weak point I had: as soon as I had started to get good reactions from girls, I would keep on doing the things that brought out more reactions. Which comes down to a very basic and deep need – we all just want to be liked.

She likes it? Good let's do more of that. However, if an interaction is to go forward, you need to stop doing what's working at the moment and try to take things to the next level. By doing that you might risk not being liked, but it doesn't matter. That's the lesson here, and that's what helped with her.

Anyway, the blonde is super hooked, so I bring her to the group and introduce her to Max, Vini, and the students. The looks on the students' eyes are almost those of disbelief. Even Max seemed impressed. Then I take her one floor down in the mall. There are no benches. I wanted to sit her down and just chat, but instead I lead like a boss and decide to go for pull, because why not.

Go back to Max, Vini and the guys with her, on the way mention that we'll have pancakes together. And guess what? The pancake place is only five minutes away! I take my jacket, grab the keys from Max (texted him in advance if it's okay), and off we go. We walk to our Airbnb, we keep chatting on the way.

So far so good.

We come close to my place, I just lead, and then say "Oh, it's here." She's surprised, but comes with me anyway. We enter, continue to chat so she feels more comfortable. Never let the uncomfortable silence linger around as you're taking the girl to your house. Lights are on when we enter, I play the music with the touch of a single button, and go take a piss while she looks around.

So far, so good.

To be honest, I'm freaking out a bit, cause she's super hot. She takes off her boots and coat, she's in a short black dress with a big V-cut so I can see her nice breasts and tight ass, long blonde hair.

DAMN she's hot. She's probably one of the hottest girls I ever pulled, if not the hottest. Like, really super fucking hot, I get kind of nervous.

Then I walk around a bit and show her the nerf gun. We'd always travel with funny props, because they are fun and because we are kids at heart. She's a bit tense. I try to get her into the smaller room, which was Vini's room (I had the floor again) which was kinda stupid. The guys were not at home and Max literally told me on several occasions he doesn't mind me using his bed if I pull.

And then after a few minutes I come closer and try to kiss her neck out of the blue.

Too early dude, what the fuck, let her breathe. Should have taken it easier, I just met her less than an hour ago, and she's at my place, in her sexy black dress and stockings.

She freaks out a bit and then says she needs to leave. I try to go for the goodbye kiss afterwards, but it doesn't work. She leaves.

"Fuck."

"FUCK!"

I'm such a fucking retard, I cannot believe what I just did. Why the fucking rush? I could be discovering that perfect body and making a connection with an amazing girl... and now I'm gonna rub my dick solo later on. The fuck.

Ah well. I'm still pretty happy, because I pulled a super hot chick, a really good reference experience.

#Reference Experience
In game, we count every single interaction, whether good or bad, as a reference experience. It's quite simple. As long as you reflect, every single reference experience, regardless of result, will make your game better.

Situations like this were previously completely out of my reality. Talk to some hot model-like blonde and just have her with you at your place in an hour. Holy shit, magic really does exist. So I was understandably freaking out a bit because I was not used to this and it probably showed; I was really nervous.

Yet, part of me was also disappointed and pissed off, because, well, I could probably have slept with her, had I stronger game. I proceed to do some video editing, whilst texting the girl from the shop before. Max and Vini just finished the Bootcamp and decided to get some food.

And then I just call the girl. Judging by her texts, it seemed she was starting to lose interest: she has a headache, needs to catch an early bus, more excuses and bullshit. So I call her, first giving her a few funny jokes, then I tell her that tonight is "our night" as I'm leaving for Helsinki the next day. She's down to meet me after that.

It's another thing I learned from Max. Texting takes time. If there's time, texting is better, less pressure for the girl, plus everybody just texts nowadays anyway. Yet, when there's no time to lose, the phone call is the last resort.

I meet her at 9pm at the mall. She closes her shop, we go out and she smokes a cigarette. Then she tries to take me to a coffee place upstairs.

"Nah, fuck that coffee place, I know a cooler place. It's five minutes away."

This sentence makes me crack up inside, it's just such a useful sentence. So we walk to my place, I point to a random bar just before our place and say:

"I wanted to take you there, but eh, what the hell, I'm sick of coffee shops, been sitting around for the whole day. I have tea at home too, it's right here, come."

This was a super good tip from Max btw - show her the bar and say you decided to go your place instead, since you were sitting in coffee places all day long. She hesitates for a bit, her bus is leaving in 15 minutes.

"Well, you can take the next one, no problem."

I lead her home, she makes a joke about a rape castle.

"Oh, I only do that on Thursdays, you're safe today."

She cracks up. We come in, this time I don't charge at her straight away; instead I make tea, turn the lights on, there's music from before. I show her my videos on the computer, and we chat for a bit in the small room.

The conversation is kinda dying out, it's a bit of a tense atmosphere. Not uncomfortable, just a bit tense. We still kinda bullshit, I ask if she can give me a massage she's like nah, not really… and then she says she needs to be going.

"Ok, that's cool…"

In my mind I'm a bit sad, but whatever. When I pulled I wasn't sure how far I can take it that night anyway, plus we'll be leaving Tallinn soon. *However, before she left I was feeling like "to hell with it, I need to try anyway." I come closer to her, to hug her goodbye.*

"I'll give you a good-bye gift."

I kiss her neck. My hands are trembling slightly. She likes the kiss, and starts to breathe heavy.

"Now kiss good-bye."

She's down, we make out. It gets a bit hot, fast. The problem is she has her coat and scarf on already. We make out again, and in a minute or so, I actually get turned on. She starts to walk towards the door.

I try to persuade her to stay.

"Look, there's more buses, right? You probably don't have to go just yet, it's not that late. What I'm saying is, we both like each other, and it's awesome. Now I'd like to spend more time with you, cuz frankly, the chance might be gone forever. Now, there's no pressure, we're not gonna do anything you're not comfortable with, just hanging out and spending some nice moments together. It's gonna be super cool and you can leave at any point."

She almost changes her mind, she touches my body for a bit, she did like those pecs, haha. And then as if she made her final decision, leaves for the door.

"Oh, before you go..."

I grab her, push her to the wall (gently) and have an even hotter make out. She loves it, but then still leaves. She was super cool about it too. I escort her out the door saying:

"Shame you're leaving."

"Don't be sad, at least you've gotten a kiss of an Estonian girl. Have a nice life!"

She leaves, and I sit on my bed with a smile. She was sweet. Yet, the smile soon disappears as I go through my interactions with women in Tallinn. I just realize I have a major case of blue balls here and it doesn't feel too good.

Jerking off helps a bit, and I soon fall asleep thinking about the whole game thing in general.

It does tend to be quite frustrating from time to time.

Chapter Five
BIGGEST FRUSTRATION AND ITS AFTERMATH

Bostjan's Private Diary Entry, Tallinn, December 2015

The heavy frustration starts here, I need to add something to the pre-story.

Rewind back one day, to Saturday, just after the Bootcamp, and I met a really cool girl. I met her during the Bootcamp, took her number, and agreed to meet her later. It was a double date with her friend and Vini, who actually kissed his girl on the way from the hotel already, and then me and my girl split in order to go to the casino.

My girl was a super cool girl. Russian, about 20 years old, and very hot. She was open-minded as well, she knew about psychology and had a really nice vibe. There was also this deep eye contact with here, and I felt like she wanted me.

We talked about a lot of topics, including open relationships, bondage sex, and other interesting topics that not everyone is willing to discuss. I liked talking to her and I wanted to fuck her badly.

So here was the situation – It was 4am, the girls came down from their hotel room to meet Vini and me. At 4 FUCKING AM, after a Saturday night out. I went to the casino together with my girl. She was okay with being away from her friend. It was her last night here, she was traveling. When I met her a few hours earlier on the Bootcamp we had a quick kiss too.

The point being, she was most probably ready to have sex that night. And I blew it. I fucked around too much in the casino. I went into a "deep discussion" with her, instead of making shit happen. I was not leading enough. I didn't cut through the shit enough. I was being too nice. So in the end, at 5am, I tried to pull her, but she wouldn't come.

I accompany her to her room after spending 2 or 3 hours in the casino. I try to squeeze myself in the room somehow, but only get a *"It was really nice to meet you, good night"* from her. That sucked really badly. Knowing you could have had HOT SEX with a beautiful girl, had you just played your cards right, sucked balls.

And then add to that the failed milf jerk off from the Tuesday. Both events built up a lot of negative emotions in me. And the end result was massive frustration.

When I went home from the Russian girl after the casino, I was so angry, I punched a wall. I literally punched a random wall on the street. With force. I bruised my knuckles.

Besides punching that wall, I was swearing loudly in Slovenian and English.

Top all of this off with the two girls that I pulled to my place the next day. Couldn't have sex with any of them either. That's 4 girls in a week I was intimate with, but could not have sex with, despite wanting it badly. Yeah, I'm a real player, the amazing assistant of RSD Max himself.

Pulls 4 girls in a week, but can't fuck any of them.

It hurt a lot, not physically, but emotionally. I am very rarely angry, maybe once every few months, think I mentioned this before. Well, this time it was hard, there's only a few moments in my life that could compare in intensity of anger to that.

And the worst part was that I was angry at myself. The burning feeling deep inside. Something beautiful could have happened, not beautiful just for me, but for the girls as well. They invested their time and energy into a guy, and he was too much of a retard to just make it happen once it was all laid down.

Basically, I was too much of a pussy to take charge, to move things further.

Such a super cool guy, good game, RSD Max's assistant, and yet I couldn't close a girl who is down to fuck. What the fuck man? How is this possible? Add this to the fact I was super horny, because I hadn't really gotten laid in Krakow either.

Sure, I have gotten some nice blowjobs, but I hadn't gotten

laid. Sex is not just penetration, in a way, it is the ultimate connection of two people, I mean, even physically. You are literally "inside" of another person. And the cuddling that normally happens after is a huge deal too.

And to top it off, once you get into game, once you become a player, getting laid sadly also becomes a measurement. For example, after you tell the guys in game that you just met this amazing girl and had an awesome time with her, one question will surely follow:

"So did you fuck her?"

It's an important question, I agree. But it's not all that matters.

And even worse, the more you are into game, the more you are in this weird *"sex-is-all-that-matters"* mindset. You start to impose it on yourself. You can have an amazing interaction with a lovely girl, and yet still feel bad after it because you didn't fuck her.

You feel like a loser, because you didn't make it happen. And the better you become, the more intense these negative feelings get. You see, because you are so "good" you kind of expect sex to happen anyway. And then when it doesn't, you feel like shit. There's this growing gap between your expectations and/or self-image, and the actual reality.

And this brings about a lot of pain.

So yeah, all these things BURNED inside of me, it was really intense. That was the most defining game moment I had in all of my travels with Max. Sounds funny, but the most powerful experience, besides hanging out with Alex, who I slowly started to fall in love with, was the frustration experience.

It taught me a lot. To take charge, to be a man. To go for it, once the situation presents itself. To feel good enough, to just feel enough. And to do it while the opportunity is there, because it might soon be gone forever.

What I didn't realize then is that this frustration is a part of the game. No matter how good you are, there are random factors. Shit like this is bound to happen. Granted, it will happen less often if your game is on point.

However, it will also burn less intensely if you don't build up too many expectations. You kind of learn how to handle those expectations, you learn to manage them with little to no repercussions. But a part of the frustration will always be there. Game inherently carries a part of frustration with it, like life does.

One cannot exist without the other, it's two sides of the same coin.

And that is something nobody tells you. That's something nobody mentions to you when you start talking to girls. I wish somebody had told me that when I was starting off:

"There's gonna be a lot of frustration, and it will suck badly. And you will need to find a way to cope with it, otherwise it will break you."

So yeah, Tallinn was quite an experience for me.

And it gave me a deeper insight into the game and the psychology as a player. I did not fully understand it then, but a realization started to form. Something that only the more mature, wise people realize.

Game, like many other things, our mind for example, is a very powerful animal. If you learn how to control it, it will help you create a wonderful life. If it's allowed to do as it will, it will break you and take you to places where there is no light.

Chapter Six
FORGOTTEN COMPUTER, ALCOHOL SMUGGLING, AND "WE'RE ON A BOAT"

Boat From Tallinn to Helsinki, December 2015

It's Monday and we're heading to Helsinki today. The difference is, we're leaving by a ferry, and not by airplane. Which is a super welcoming change. A bit of difference to our routine, plus we don't have to spend the whole day at the airport.

So we get some nice sleep in, pack our shit, and leave the Airbnb. Another Monday morning, another travel day. Then Max calls an Uber to bring us to the port. In the Uber I remember Max talking about his past metal band days, when he was actually on tour before, albeit with a much smaller following. Back then, he tried to get with (metalhead) girls too, but it was more difficult, because he was more or less a chode himself.

We arrive at the port and sort out our tickets. I watch over our gear, while Max and Vini take a piss. Mind you, there was a suitcase with camera equipment worth of about $20,000, and then all our computers and other stuff easily amounted to another $10,000. So when I say I watched the gear, I mean it. Max made really sure that we kept an eye on our things all the time. It's become a habit.

For example, even long after the tour, I still double check if I have my bag with me every single time I leave a car, a plane, or a train.

But anyway, I was quite bored, so I chat up some girl. She was hot, but it doesn't go too well so I don't even get her details. And then the guys come back shortly after. We are about to head to the boat and then Vini asks me:

"Dude, where is your backpack?"

"Fuck."

"FUCK."

I start breathing heavy and get really stressed, really fast. The only thing that is keeping me sane is the compulsive obsession on thinking out the best course of action to get the backpack back ASAP.

I search the place, think hard, and realize it's still in the Uber.

And you see, in my backpack, I had a number of valuable things. My passport, a decent amount of cash, and my work computer - a MacBook Pro, which Max had gotten for me to use while I worked for him. The worst thing? I had a lot of saved projects and important data on that computer, data and videos that were probably worth more than the computer in the long run.

If I didn't get that backpack back, I was fucked. FUCKED.

But all hail the Uber app, which had anticipated situations like this. Thanks to the app, I soon get the number of the driver, I call him and arrange for him to come back to the port. He brings my bag and I'm so happy I drop a 20€ note into his hands. I'm getting short on cash, and I know it's not much compared to the value of my gear, but at least I covered his time.

Then we roll to the ferry (we're still on time, luckily), and I see something funny. A lot of the people going to the ferry, have shopping trolleys with them. And the trolleys are loaded with alcohol. Cases of beer, huge numbers of vodka and wine bottles. It's like every second person is carrying some alcohol with them.

I talk to some people and realize that alcohol is A LOT cheaper in Estonia than in Finland. So people come to Tallinn by ferry, which is 20€ and two hours away. And then they load up on the alcohol supply, because the price difference is ridiculous. I think a 4-pack of beer is like a 3-4€ in Tallinn, and like €12 in Helsinki. IN A SHOP!

So yeah, in the midst of all the alcohol trolleys and some drunk people, we hang out on the boat. And I'm not sure if it was Max or Vini who played it, but one of them played the song called *"I'm on a Boat."*

A super funny moment - we're chilling on a boat, the boat song is playing in the background, and Max is firing up the Periscope app.

Periscope is a social media app, it's kinda like putting yourself on YouTube, but live. Same as Facebook live, or YouTube live. By the time you're reading this book, you probably know about these apps anyway, and Periscope might be dying out.

"Hello friends, welcome to this Periscope session, thanks for dropping by, I really appreciate it! Right now, as you can hear in the back, I'm on a boat and heading off to Helsinki."

He puts his broadcasting phone near Vini's which is still playing the song. We all start rapping/singing to the song.

"I'm on a boat motherfucker, I'm on a boat. Everybody look at me, cuz I'm sailing on a boat..."

We are all laughing our asses off, and Max continues:

"So anyway people, glad to have you here and sharing this moment with us. As you know, it's time for our daily Periscope session, so shoot me some questions and I'll answer them."

The little heart symbols of people liking what Max is saying start to pop up. There's about 150 viewers online at the time. Max starts reading out the questions:

Yo Max, how do I get into game again after a long break? I was with my girlfriend and stopped gaming and now it's over, It's really tough.

"Hey my friend, this sucks, it's true. Lucky for you, I made a

whole video about it, type into YouTube "RSD Max, how to get back into game after a break" and thank me later."

Hey Max, find a girl close to you and tell her I love her.

"Haha, sorry bro, no girls around at the moment."

Max, when are you coming to Mexico?

"No plans for there yet my friend, however, I will be in Miami in February."

Hey Max, I want to talk to girls but I'm afraid, what do I do?

"Hey my friend, yeah, you'll just have to overcome this, I made a whole video about it, type into YouTube "RSD Max approach anxiety" and thank me later."

Hey Max, who's holding the camera, Vinny or Bostyan?

"It's Bostjan at the moment bro, but Vini's here too!"

So cool, some of Max's fans really loved him a lot, they even knew our names and Max didn't really drop them that often. But it felt kinda cool, somebody you don't know knows who you are, and wonders what you're doing. But they always misspelled our names, haha.

Hey Max, I went out solo after watching your "How to talk to girls alone" video and then pulled an awesome blonde girl, thanks so much man!

"Hey bro, I'm really glad to hear that, good fucking job man!"

And so it continued for about 30 minutes. People would ask him questions, and he'd answer them. And it was a mix, you know, a lot of the questions were about game, or healthy lifestyle, or work ethic, but some were also pretty personal. Which video games Max likes, what his favorite guitar solo was, etc.

And what I noticed at that moment is that Max really cared about his fans. He shared a lot of personal stories with them, and also gave a lot of really good advice, for free. Keep in mind, an hour Skype consultation with him costs hundreds of dollars, and a 3-day bootcamp is thousands.

It's not easy to log into Periscope or YouTube live every day, and share with your fanbase. But he did that. And not just with the social media. That was Max's way. Always do a little bit more, squeeze the last drop out. And he'd try to do that every single day.

My respect for him grew and grew, and even after months, I was still learning new things every day.

Chapter Seven
I AM A PIMP - I FUCK UGLY GIRLS

Helsinki, December 2015

So we arrived to Helsinki around 7pm.

I dropped the bags with Max and Vini, and then went to find my host. It was really cold already. I took a selfie pic when I was in the centre and posted it on Facebook. My nose was really red, yet I had a big smile on my face. I felt happy. A new city, new adventures. The tiredness was masked, at least for a few moments.

I go meet my host, a super cool dude. For a Finnish guy, amazingly open and talkative. I say this not only because of the stereotype, but Finnish people, and guys even more so, really are a bit more reserved. We chat for a bit, then I go meet Max and do some video editing. At around 1am I head home, I drop my bag off, and then head back out to a club suggested to me by my earlier host from Krakow, a buddy who was actually Finnish.

A super weird thing happened to me that night, one that would make me reflect on this whole game thing even more.

The club where I go is more or less a shit hole, but no worries. I'm used to those by now. I'm pretty tired, but I still have the killer instinct. I see my buddy in set and drop in to say hi. I was totally too high energy, but I didn't care because I was happy to see him again, so the girls gave me a weird look.

After I said hi to my buddy from Krakow, I left the set. However, being an awesome wing, while going away, said to the girl with a smile:

"Hey, be nice to my friend, I'm watching you!"

Such a great line to boost up your wing's social value, learned it from Max, of course. I continue through the club, silently, slowly, kind of like a sniper, but with a lazy grin on my face. I knew what I was searching for. I see two girls sitting...

The merry-go-round goes round and round...

I talk to a lot of girls that night, I don't even remember how many. I remember an interaction with a super hot girl from Miami, and a few others. My game is really good that night, a lot of the girls hooked, I grabbed some contacts, had a make out, etc.

And I realize how good my game had become recently. I'd never, even in my wildest dreams, think that I could just fly in in a country, go to some club the same night, start pimping, and have girls love me, kiss me, and just interact with me so effortlessly. It was slowly becoming a part of my reality. I recognized the almost bored grin on my face, I've seen it before...

But that was not good enough for me. I was on a sex mission that night, I really wanted to get laid. Not sure if it was the hormones, or the whole frustration from Tallinn, or a mix of everything.

However, somehow, none of the girls were down enough. Either they had work the next day, or they needed to leave with friends, or they had boyfriends. Something was there that would just not allow them to have sex with me that night. And this happens in game, sometimes you just don't get laid, and that's cool.

In retrospective, it seems I was entering a weird, almost manic-like state during those times, sex really did matter to me. A lot. The club closed, and I still didn't have any girl I could bang that night, fuck.

Cool, let's try the door game.

Door Game
When the club is closing or about to close. You leave the club and linger around close to the front door. When girl come out, you just chat them up, screening if they might be down for an after party or food.

Sometimes, you can still get a girl that is exiting the club to come with you, or vice versa. Guys have been hitting on her all night, they've been buying her drinks. She's been dancing and having fun. She was out on a Monday night, she was probably down to meet a cool guy.

But only if he was really cool, and only if she could do it without anyone judging her. Yet, nobody pulled the trigger. She's also horny, she wants to get laid too. It's not just us guys that feel like that sometimes. It doesn't always happen, but I guess it's worth a shot.

I open some two-set as we are leaving the club together, my buddy in the back coming to join in. The girl I like only speaks Finnish and Russian, fuck, we start to make half-assed plans for an afterparty. Somebody mentions weed and then another girl exits the club. She is walking by herself, and I ask:

"Excuse me, do you have some weed?" She hooks instantly, gives me the Bambi eyes, and says: *"No weed."*

"Ok, how about you show me where I can get some food at this time. I'm new here."

"My place."

Well, that's a first, I think to myself. She's kinda straight forward. *"Aha ok, let's go."*

I offer her my arm and off we go. I still kind of can't believe it. I didn't even know her, and after a sentence, we were walking hand in hand, apparently to her place. Is this some sort of magic, am I missing something, what's happening?

We just walk for about 20 minutes and chat, I tell her I'm just being a gentleman by walking her home. She's staying at some hotel not far away. She's not super hot to be honest, yet I am excited by what's happening. I don't even "game" much, I just listen to her, smalltalk, and share some of my thoughts.

Arm holding is super good as I feel her squeezing my

biceps, I guess she was as horny as I was that night. We arrive at the hotel, I ask whether I can use the toilet and she's cool with that. We get to her room and then the 2nd surprise follows. We see two of her friends, naked in the bed (a guy and a girl).

It seems like they just finished fucking not long ago. I laugh really hard. My girl is half-angry, half-happy for her friend. So they all hug and shout random shit in Finnish. The funny thing is, it wasn't awkward I was there. In most countries her friends would start to ask who I am, etc, yet in Finland it was cool. She found some player dude who will fuck her, and that's cool. Then my girl kicks them out. They leave half-naked, trying to get dressed as soon as possible. What a funny sight.

And then we fuck.

It wasn't that amazing, to be honest, She wasn't so hot, and we didn't find the right rhythm for quite some time. Even kissing her was not awesome. But it felt good. At least until I came. Then I felt kind of empty, and didn't really cuddle that much. Luckily I was tired, so I got sleepy fast.

She drinks some water, I take a pic of her ass and send it to Vini and Max and then fall asleep. I was mad tired, no wonder, it was my first day in Helsinki. In the morning I wake her up via fingering her and we have sex again; this time it was better. Soon after, some workers start to drill in the hotel, so I kiss her goodbye and get the hell out, go to my place and fall asleep again.

After I wake up, I check the picture I sent to the guys again. And some weirdly dark, doubtful thoughts start to emerge.

The girl was not the type of a girl I would walk around with. She was not attractive in my standards. I wouldn't spend time with her. I wouldn't bring her to meet my friends. I wouldn't take her out. So why the hell did I hook up with her? Just because I was horny and wanted to put my dick somewhere?

And funny enough, even the sex itself was not amazing. Yes, we were both horny, but she was not really that attractive to me and there was practically no connection as well.

So if it was not for the sex, and if it was not for her, why the fuck did I want to bang her so much? It got me thinking.

What's the whole point of picking up ugly girls who you don't feel deeply for? All of a sudden, it all seemed so alien to me. Every free night, I would go out to some bar or club, like a crazed vulture searching for prey. I would basically fuck anything that wanted me.

I realized that part of me did it just because I was horny, it's natural. There's a lot of jokes about guys who hook up with an ugly girl due to alcohol and only realize that in the morning. And it's similar for girls. Sometimes they sleep with a dude simply because they're horny. They don't plan to date him or see him again. It's cool. It happens.

But for me, the rabbit hole ran deeper. A part of me was already caught in the player identity, where you only value yourself if you get laid consistently. As long as you pull and get laid, you're a good player. If you don't, you suck. Your game sucks. You are not a player at all. Your identity starts to crumble...

Again, the connection, the fun and playful vibe, the sharing of personal stories. None of that matters to a guy lost in this dark aspect of the game. The only question that matters is: *"But did you fuck her?"*

And it's kinda sad.

Why do we place so much importance on the sex thing? I mean, sex is cool, it feels good, obviously. But it's not all that matters. I started to game to have girls I like around me, to have a nice girlfriend, or a few.

Girls who loved me for who I am. To be unafraid of expressing how I feel, to go talk to a girl I like and tell her that. To try to get to know her and vice versa.

So how come these innocent and healthy needs and wishes got so twisted in the process of becoming a player, without me even realizing it? How is this possible? I'm probably in the top percent of guys in game. I'm not near Max's level yet, but I'm much closer than the regular gaming dude. Why do I feel so weird and confused then?

Did I start to get really good with women? Yes.

But it seemed there were some serious "side effects" too.

And the rabbit hole just ran deeper and deeper...

Chapter Eight
DARKNESS, NO EVENTS, DEPRESSION

Helsinki, December 15

The week in Helsinki was supposed to be pretty chill; we had no Bootcamp this time. Funnily enough, you only get to feel how tired you are, when you actually slow down and take a breath. I was kind of conserving energy wherever I could. I'd skip a flight of stairs if I could. I'd buy a pre-made sandwich instead of cooking. It was way worse for Max and Vini.

We had more free time, but couldn't really use it to be more productive. Normally we'd shoot a video blog for Max in every city. Well, not in Helsinki – we just shot the intro. We'd still hit the gym, but way less than we used to.

Max came up with an idea of playing computer games.

"Yo, Bostjan. After you buy the groceries today, I have a special task for you. Find a computer store and buy 3 mouses, one for you, one for me, and one for Vini. I have a sick idea!"

So I come to his and Vini's Airbnb with the mouses, and then we all install *'Command & Conquer Zero Hour – Generals.'* Max buys subscription for all of us, so we can play in multiplayer mode, and then we get down to business.

I was pretty excited to be honest, the game was a strategic warfare game, similar to the *Red Alert 2* which I used to play as a kid ALL THE TIME. I mean seriously, all the time. Hours upon hours.

You see, the funny thing with computer games is, time flies. Some of today's games, especially the MMORPGs, or Mass Multiplayer Online Role Playing Game, such as *World of Warcraft* or others, are so good, you get addicted. Seriously, it's crazy. You can literally play the game for 10 hours a day for months and not get bored. And once you do get bored, you just get a new game.

Fun? Yes.

Dangerous? Yes.

Anyway, we play C & C for a few hours, and since we were done with the video editing for the day, I decided to go hit a club with my host instead of playing more games. The guys stayed in.

In fact, the whole week, I was still going out whenever I could, but Max and Vini would just stay in. They would not go out and pimp it, even though they both love game. We would work a lot, as before, but the time we usually spent running the Bootcamp would now be used to play computer games and sleep.

On one hand I understood that a recharge was needed, but when you play Command & Conquer till 7am a few days in a row and sleep in until 3pm, it's a sign that not everything is right.

Things were getting weird, and I wasn't sure what to think of the sudden computer games obsession with Max. But, I didn't pay much heed to it. I had some more time off, which only happened 2 or 3 weeks in the whole tour, so I was very happy to discover the city and pimp it. Just a shame Max and Vini wouldn't join me...

One day Max went on a Tinder date though.

He came back in a few hours, around 2 am, and we played some C & C, since I was done with the editing for the day and not pimping it. After the game, I asked him how the Tinder date was.

"Yeah, she was really cool man. An older girl, super good vibe, sexy, smart. I wanted to go to hers straight, but she wouldn't, so we grabbed a drink in a bar. I got kinda drunk after 2 glasses of wine, you know how I don't drink, haha.

And then we went to hers and well, we ended up having sex pretty fast. She totally clawed my back, haha. But yeah, she was really cool, we cuddled and talked too. And she told me I look overworked and all, and she was kind of right. She does some sort of energy healing stuff for work, it was quite interesting."

And I could see on his face that the girl really was pretty cool, he kind of liked her. Yet, when I asked him if he will meet her again, he said:

"Nah, I already fucked her."

I didn't quite understand that then. Now, in retrospective, I can accept it, but it's still something I cannot understand. I'd later come to a point where game would lose its appeal too, but never this far. Or maybe it was a personal thing, I don't know. But I doubt it.

And I never could get it why some guys would only have sex with a girl once. I mean, okay, if they were super drunk, and that messed with their perception, I guess I can understand. But at least for me, if I like a girl enough to sleep with her, I'd like to do that on at least several occasions, not just once.

So basically, the whole atmosphere was getting pretty grim in my mind. I was getting confused and not sure what to think about the game anymore. I was starting to get some real results, finally, yet my perception and emotions were starting to get fucked over by a large, dark shadow I could not name.

Not that the weather outside helped with that. It was dark, really cold, and there was no sun after 3 or 4pm. Drizzling or raining most of the time, not many people on the streets due to cold, and just general heaviness in the air.

Even in the guys' Airbnb (I was still staying with my host) the atmosphere was grim and dark. As if something was sucking the energy out of you. A place where motivation just gets drained out of you, a place where you just want to kill time and make it pass faster. All Max would want to do after work is play Command & Conquer and sleep.

I didn't want to hang around there too much unless I had

to.

I remember the story of Max and Vini getting drunk with the Airbnb welcome champagne one night. Well, it didn't take much. 2 glasses each was quite enough, based on what they told me, haha. And then some C & C after. However, I was not there at the time, I was pimping it. Which is probably good, because I had to escape the bad vibes.

There was just a huge lack of initiative. Looking back, I'm surprised we even handled the Hot Seat and the Free Tour as we did. However, Max did seem to get some more life back into him when talking at the Free Tour. As if it brought a bit of life back to him, or better, as if that was the only thing keeping him going.

On one hand, I was quite happy, because I would have time to pimp. I went out quite a lot that week, both with my host and the previous host from Krakow, who was here now. I saw the city, I got laid twice (yes, I'll explain). However, whenever I got back to Max and Vini's Airbnb, it felt as though something was wrong.

Come down the hole with me...

Chapter Nine
DAT ASS LAY REPORT

Helsinki Inner Circle Facebook Group

Lay Report

On Wednesday I went out with my host again. We went to some student place, an amazing big club in the centre of Helsinki. The entry fee was 15€, which hurt a little as my funds were getting low.

My game had been super on point recently, those mind fucks and frustrations in Tallinn actually helped, even though they were really cruel. But yeah, my game was probably the best it ever had been. It was quite crazy for me to have such a level of calmness and no fear.

I could talk to anyone I wanted to, which up to this point had never been the case. I felt like I had super powers. I would almost always know exactly what to say and what to do. I had a really good feel of how much a girl liked me and how likely it was that something will happen. More or less the only problem I had was a bit of nervousness with really hot girls.

We pop inside. The club is amazing. Big venue, several floors, lots of silent areas for verbal game, and super, SUPER hot girls. Anywhere you turn, you have these beautiful women, blonde, brunette, slender, with beautiful bodies and faces. Nature did something really good here.

Welcome to Finland.

So as soon as I see a hot chick, which is literally the first set I see (a two-set), I open straight away. She hooks. Chat for a bit, yet I was a little too playful, and then kinda fucked it up so I move on.

I open a few more sets, but nothing amazing happens. I pop to the dance floor. I rarely dance nowadays, only if I really like the music or really feel like dancing. What I do instead is, I stand in the middle or in the corner of the dance floor and observe. I take my time, breathe, and check which girls I like.

And a funny thing happens. If you are calm, and just standing there, people, girls will start to look over. What's up with that guy? Why is he just standing there with a smile on his face? That's intriguing to them.

However, it doesn't work if you just stand there because you're too afraid to move, dance, or go talk to someone. It has to be real. You actually have to be there and just chill, until you want to do something else, like dancing, or talking to some girl. Might sound funny, but that's how it is.

Soon I spot two hotties, so I go straight to them, look them in the eye, and open. Both of them hook. The one I open doesn't really understand me (lack of English) so I shift to the other one, who is hotter too. Taller than me, super skinny, long dark curls, ring-

piercing in her nose, 20 years old. She was a head-turner, I could see the eyes of people around me checking me out as I approached them.

Anyway, both girls are super happy, so I chill for a bit with them, then I say let's go smoke and lead them to the quieter area. I just show them to some chairs instead, we sit down. They don't even ask me why we didn't go to the smoking area. It just gets effortless after some time.

I chat to them both and they both love me. I was first thinking I needed a wing, but then said to myself, "fuck it, let's test the waters for a threesome."

"So girls, have you ever kissed each other?"

They seem pretty disgusted, which is obviously not cool, so I don't push it into that direction any more.

Turns out the hotter brunette who I've now chosen is single and the friend has a boyfriend, perfect. Logistics are not too bad, they are free next day, but live pretty far. So I chill with these two girls for an hour and a half. In between my buddy wings for some time and I handle both girls at other times.

The interaction with both was really good, especially with the brunette. She was asking a lot of questions, explaining herself and her actions, in general contributing a lot to the interaction. I knew I had to move things forward.

So at some point I lead her to a more intimate place by pulling the best trick ever.

Her friend, who was chatting with my buddy, protested when I told her that I'll borrow her friend for a few minutes. So I take off my wrist watch and hand it to her:

"Time me, I'll bring her back in two minutes, I promise. And in the meantime, my friend will keep you company."

They all laugh and it's cool for us to go. "Like a boss."

We come to the quieter lounge area, I sit her down. She becomes a bit uncomfortable, which I feel. I chat with her for a minute, but then still go for the make out despite intuition. I knew I was pushing it a little bit, but then again, I didn't want to risk falling into the friend zone by not making a move. The interaction was quite long already.

She refuses to kiss me and asks me to take her back. I take her back and ask her on the way:

"Was I too quick?"

"Yes."

Now, I do get this type of reaction with certain girls, usually girls who I like and also girls who are a bit closed, you know, girls who have a lot of walls put up, who are not super sexually open from the start. So yeah, I feel that interaction kind of went to hell, which is a shame. She was a really cool girl, I liked her, and she was super hot too.

We still chill together, she gives me typical bullshit from then on:

"Just find another girl tonight, you just want to have sex."

Well, can't blame her, she's kind of right, haha. Explaining that wanting sex and being open about it is actually pretty cool probably won't work with her. 90 minutes or so in, I take down her number while making plans for later and then do, in fact, leave her to find some other girl who is down.

I guess I followed her advice, haha.

I am really proud of this decision too. Back in the day I would bask in the presence of a hottie, stay there forever, and in the end just blow it anyway. I'd stay, despite knowing nothing else is gonna happen that night. She would start to feel that she means the world to me after meeting me only once. And that's not a major turn on for a girl.

Anyway, I'm on my way, it's getting late, about 2 or 3am. I open two more sets, nothing hooks, so I go past the dance floor and see a girl sitting alone, checking her phone. "Ka-ching!" A girl checking her phone alone in the club in a visible place clearly wants to be approached. I mean, she might also be wasted or sad because all her friends left her, but more often, she's just open to be approached.

I "Cheers" open her, and she hooks instantly. A bit of bullshit, she has a good sense of humor and is away from her absent friends. I figure she is completely DTF. I take her to the lounge and then chill for a min, then make out with her and then pull back so she wants more. Same old story, it's kind of getting boring.

She is hooked on me like I was cocaine, haha. She can't believe I'm teasing her so hard and she's absolutely loving it. Touching me everywhere, almost begging me to kiss her more. One mistake I did was to kiss her in the same area where the hot brunette from before was. I think she saw me making out with this blonde girl. Damn. Ah well, whatever.

After that I take her to the dance floor, we dance a bit, I make her chase, dance for a bit, and kiss more. After that it's the silent area again, a bit of talking and more kissing. We make plans for pancakes - seeding the pull. Her logistics are fucked, mine aren't too good either: my host specifically said no pulling back to his, it's a one bedroom flat and I'm crashing on the floor.

My host is working in the morning too and it's now Wednesday at 3am. We talk pretty openly about where to go, plus she doesn't mention her friends. Got to love Finland. Women are really independent here and in general don't give much of a crap regarding societal pressure and slut shaming.

She is super down and probably dripping wet by this time. Oh, she's pretty hot too, great body, blonde, blue eyes. Your typical Finnish cutie. She wasn't a stunning head turner like the last brunette girl, but she was definitely hot.

Then we walk towards the bus, the plan was to go to her place; she's far, but has her own room. We vibe and have a good time on the way. For example, we play "the questions" game.

It's a really fun game, and super easy. You ask the other person any question you want, and they have to answer, or in extreme cases say "pass." It usually starts off gentle, questions about family, hobbies, random things, and then proceeds to questions such as what is your biggest sexual fantasy, etc.

She's super chill, I remember we both piss in some corner at some point and then talk more about a lot of things including the Lord of the Rings, video games, my threesome experience from Lithuania, and more. So yeah, the only thing I needed to do is lead the interaction and not fuck it up. However, her bus is at 5am. It's now 4am, no way we can wait outside for an hour, it was freezing.

Fuck it.

I take her to my place, even though the host sleeps above us in the loft. I made that decision because she was super cool and I knew there would be no drama with her. So we arrive, I whisper that we should get into our underwear and cuddle, she's down.

The moment I am next to her, on my mat on the floor, I start kissing her. It's crazy, this is one of the most intensive sex experiences I had on the tour. It got super hot, super fast. And the best thing about it was, we had to be SUPER quiet because we could hear our host gently snoring upstairs. It's really sexy.

Everything is dark, there's a little bit of light from the street lights outside. I kiss her passionately, and my hands are all over her. I can feel her boobs rubbing against me, and when I grasp her ass with my hands she quietly moans. Very soon, I touch her pussy and find out she is dripping wet. She just gives me a naughty smile and starts rubbing my dick.

"Come on, fuck me now, I am so horny, I want you dick deep inside of me."

I don't make her beg, I take the condom, rip it out of the paper, put it on, and penetrate her deeply.

Usually, I'd do the first thrust slow, but in this case, I was so turned on I pushed it in all the way. It felt so amazing, so hot, so deep. It was perfect. A semi-loud gasp escapes her mouth as I do this, and I put my hand on her mouth, as to keep her quiet.

She is biting my hand and later on my neck as I am fucking her harder. Slow and deep strokes is what I'm doing, because that produces the least amount of noise. I can feel her hips shifting from left to right below me and I feel I will come very soon, this is just so good.

I have this perfect image in my mind. Both of us on the floor, next to the heater below the window, with my host sleeping just a few metres away. Me penetrating her deeply, and then her body shaking violently as she has an orgasm. She bit my hand really hard at that point. The whole thing turned me on so much, I came at the same time.

We fall asleep soon after.

We have to wake up about two hours later because there is an electrician coming. Also there is a slightly awkward situation when my host wakes to see us there, bundled together on the floor. My girl is so shy now, and hiding under the sleeping bag as he comes to say hi. But the guy was super cool about it, so mad respect to him!

We take the metro to her place straight after. She has a nice student room, with a mattress on the floor. It was about 9am, so it was getting lighter. I was really sleep-deprived, yet I could see how sexy her body really is. I get very horny and very hard again. I kiss her passionately, and all of our clothes fly off. This time we had some music and we could be loud.

Her ass was just so perfect, tight, beautiful. As I was fucking her from behind, I tried to put my finger in her ass. I saw pure fire in her eyes, she was loving it, she moaned hard. I push the finger all the way in and she starts to be really loud. Soon after, without any lubricant, I fuck her right in the ass. This was so fucking hot.

I think she came several times, and when my turn came, she even let me come on her face, this was just an epic, sexy, beautiful experience.

We then sleep for another two hours and wake up around 11.

I shit you not, I was immediately horny again, so we have sex one more time. This time the sex was really good too, I ate her pussy, she gave me an awesome blowjob, and even massaged my balls and cock after I came. I love it when girls know how to take care of you properly.

After that we grab some breakfast in a shop, and make plans to meet later that week.

I leave with the familiar big grin on my face, full of wonder and excitement.

I was 100% certain I will see her again. There was not a shadow of doubt in my mind. There's no chance in hell I will not meet her again, not after the amazing night that we spent together.

Yet this is exactly what happened...

Chapter Ten
FUCKING FLAKES

Sunday Evening

Last day in Helsinki, we're off to Gothenburg, Sweden the next day.

After the initial texting the same day, the hot ass blonde from Wednesday stopped responding.

"What the fuck?" We had an awesome time, awesome connection, fucked like porn stars, and now she's not responding? *Like what the actual fuck?*

She responds a day or two later, but super short, and again stops responding when I'm trying to schedule a meet up. The last time she answers to my text from Sunday afternoon was a few days later, when I was already in Sweden.

This made me feel really bad. How could this happen? We obviously had a great time together. She laughed a lot, and I could see how happy she was around me. We had amazing sex, we both had several orgasms. And then when I want to meet up with her again, not only is she not down, she doesn't even respond to my texts.

And that's the thing with flakes that sometimes people just don't understand. It fucking sucks.

You were getting ready to see the person you fancied again. Maybe you had a plan of what the two of you could do, how it would be to talk again, to laugh again. How it would be to touch again, to have awesome, wild sex. All these hopes, feelings, thoughts. Obliterated.

And not even by a *"No, sorry, I can't meet you because this or that."* Just radio silence. That's just plain cruel. Like, what the fuck am I supposed to make of it? Guess what went wrong, have doubts about myself, my actions? Is it me, is it her? Fuck, this is really frustrating.

Maybe she fucks a lot of guys and it's not a big deal for her. Maybe our "connection" was not that special after all, or it was, but only to me. Maybe there was something else I didn't notice. Maybe it was her problem and she was afraid of getting attached. Maybe she had some other issues at the moment. I can't say. But I know it hurt a lot at the time. I thought I had something beautiful, and I just got blatantly robbed without any explanation.

See, this time (like many others), I was absolutely sure I would see her again. 100% positive. We even took selfies, made future plans, everything; it was almost like a boyfriend-girlfriend thing. Well, not exactly, but it was really cool and warm. I could see myself spend a lot of time with that girl, she was funny, we were both kind of geeks, she was hot. I guess it didn't go two ways.

So yeah, that was another one of those frustrations,

another fucking flake. And all those flakes started to pile up. A few flakes in every city sum up to a lot of flakes in a few months. A lot of tiny cuts to the heart. Pile them on top of each other, and you get a recipe for disaster.

Oh, just to add, the other girl, that brunette I spent 90 minutes in the club with, she flaked too. She wouldn't meet me either. Vini tried to help me to turn the texting game around with her, and get her interested again, but somehow, it was not enough, she would just not meet me.

See, Sunday afternoons were a little more chill, and after work I loved it (all of us guys did) if I could have a date in the evening. Bask in feminine energy, enjoy a few hours off with a girl. Relax a bit, let go of all the hustle and work.

And it hadn't happened that much recently. Even though my game was really solid, even though I fucked two different girls that week. I got plenty of numbers, make outs, attraction, and attention from beautiful girls all around.

The truth is, inside, I was getting frustrated and sad.

Welcome to the dark side of the game...

Chapter Eleven
DARK DAYS, DARK TIMES

Gothenburg, December 2015

The last city of this part of the tour was Gothenburg, Sweden. It was around the 20th of December, Christmas was coming. Christmas is such a family holiday, I was remembering this time of the year back in Slovenia.

We'd go to church, we'd have a nice Christmas dinner, all the family would gather. Well, for the last few years we'd have two nice Christmas dinners, since my parents are divorced, but you get what I mean. It was a very warm and relaxing time.

Even when I was abroad as an exchange student in Lithuania a few years ago, I was amidst my friends, and we had a great big dinner. I had a girl or two in my life at the time so I could share some love, affection, and intimacy. Yes, that includes sex. Again, a warm and relaxing atmosphere.

Last year was worse, I was in London, working with the aggressive kids. But even that was pretty good, we still had a Christmas dinner. Yes, I was working on Christmas Day because it was double pay and because I had no real friends to spend Christmas with in the UK yet. And it still felt warm and nice, even though the kids had a few fights.

And this year, around Christmas time?

I was in fucking Sweden. It was cold as fuck, suffocatingly dark, and I hadn't seen the sun for weeks. Furthermore, I was working my ass off and was starting to get really tired. And I was still not getting paid, in fact, I was burning my own money, and was down to about a third of what I had started with.

To top it all off, the girl thing was getting a bit weird too. I chased after girls like a mad dog, and started to get results and experiences every player would be proud of. Yet, despite getting laid pretty often and having all these stories, I couldn't get the proximity I really wanted. I couldn't experience the warmth, the connection, the intimacy.

I guess what I really wanted was to caress a girl. To hold her tightly through the night, to wake up next to her, or to wake her up with a kiss. To fuck her passionately, just the way she wanted to, and then to experience eternity with her in a few orgasmic moments.

Instead, I received flake, after flake, after flake. One frustration after another. Meet a girl, try to hang out with her more than once, and get flaked on again.

FUCKING FLAKES! What the fuck is wrong with me?

What the fuck is wrong with my game, with the game, with everything? This fucking sucks, big time, and I'm not sure if I want to do this anymore.

I mean, looking back, obviously I was super busy and only in town for a week, so it was kind of unrealistic to expect I could meet the same girl several times. But I still wanted to. Some of the girls I met were really cool and I wanted to spend more time with them.

Guess not.

So you see my personal struggle was starting to get bigger, and the emotional side was way worse than the physical which was pretty fucked up too. As I said, I'm tough, I can take a beating well, emotionally and physically, yet this was an odyssey like nothing I had ever experienced.

And to top it off, Max was dropping into a deep and dark, weird, depressive state too. Like seriously, it got really bad in Gothenburg.

He stopped going to the gym. He kept on asking me to find some weed. All he wanted to do was to play Command & Conquer and just smoke all day. He was eating shit food too. Sugar, Doritos, microwaved bullshit. And not just once-a-month on a cheat day. Almost every day.

He stopped chasing girls, even Tinder was left more or less untouched. Maybe he'd text some girls to have a bit of a banter, but he wouldn't go to actually meet them, at least not in Gothenburg.
We didn't film any videos in Gothenburg. We stopped with the editing too. And you have to understand something; for Max, work was religion. Once he stopped hustling, you

could tell something was really wrong. It's the first time I'd seen him in this kind of light, and it was not pretty.

Good thing Max had at least 10 videos finished, all up and ready to be published as a backup, so his brand didn't suffer. But yeah, it was going downhill really fast.

Even the energy in the flat was grim and evil; it was a long time ago, but I remember as vividly as if it had happened yesterday. I'd came from my host to the Airbnb, and I saw Max and Vini. Both had dark faces, were doing some stuff on the computer. The energy was foreboding and draining, it felt really heavy in my chest. I felt Max had lost all the drive and willpower. It's hard to explain this with words, but I felt like he was a mini black hole sucking the positivity out of me.

I think Vini joined me for shopping once and we had a chat about this. I asked him how he thought Max was doing. I told him that I thought Max was really depressed and burnt out. I remember having watched a video of him having a burnout in Vegas a year or so ago. He looked similar, but it was even worse now.

Vini agreed that it was similar to this, and that this time it might be even worse. He didn't like it either. He had enough of his own shit to carry, and getting a load of bad vibes from Max didn't help either. We felt bad about that, bad for Max.

But we agreed that if it continued, we needed to get the hell away from it. No tour, no game advice, nothing is worth being in the presence of such a negative energy. Don't take me wrong, Max is one of the most inspirational people I've ever met in my life, I call him "bro" and I really mean it. I have his back and he's got mine.

However, shit got so bad it was getting too dark, too dangerous. And if I learned one thing in therapy it's this:

"You can't help anyone or do anything good, if you are empty and in a dark place yourself."

And I felt that the more time I spent around him, the more drained I felt. Might sound dickish, but I didn't like coming to the flat that week and I tried to avoid it as much as possible. Get the bare logistics and work done, and then get the hell out of it.

Chapter Twelve
THE GOTHENBURG MONEY TALK

I had a money talk with Max in Gothenburg.

I had been preparing myself for the talk a lot. I bailed out one time when I had a great opportunity. I didn't bring it up, I chickened out. I felt a similar way to when you don't talk to that hot girl when you have the option to, it fucking sucks. You disappoint yourself. And the thing with missed opportunities is, they never get any better.

So the second time I had the opportunity to start it, it was much harder because Vini was present. And make no mistake, I trust him fully, and we're good friends, but this was a business talk, and it added pressure. And on top of everything, I felt bad for Max too. I knew he was feeling like shit, so I didn't want to add to his load either, but fuck it, you have to put yourself first. You can't share and give to the world if you're empty yourself...

"Yo Max, can we talk about something?"

"Sure, what's up, bro?"

At this point, we knew each other really well. I guess I said that sentence in a serious way. So Max turned his face from the computer towards me, repositioned a little in his seat and started to listen. Kind of like a silent encouragement; *"I know you want to say something important, I'm here, I'm listening, so say it."*

"I'd like to talk to you about the flights, about the travels. It's getting expensive man, and my money is running out."

"Now look, I'll be really honest. I'm having the time of my life, I'm learning stuff, I'm traveling, I'm doing cool shit, it's really, really awesome. But, I don't want to be broke after. I still have some money, and I have something coming in from the remote work I do. But it's not enough. So I'm asking you to help me out. Could you start paying for my travels? At least for the USA part, because they cost more."

"I know it's tricky, because we agreed on me doing everything voluntarily. And I know that you can get another assistant just like that, who would willingly come and work for you and pay for all his expenses. However, I'll say one thing. You know they would not be as good as me."

"I've been recording pretty sick infields for you, I'm doing the censoring, I manage your groceries, plus a lot of other things. I know how to set up the rooms for the Free Tour and the Hot Seat; basically, I learned how to do my work, which is making your life much easier, really well."

"So look, I'm pretty sure the next guy won't be as good. And on top of that, you'd need to train him again. Show him the ropes again, trust him again. And that takes a lot of effort from your

side, a lot of time, I know that. And as you always say, your time costs a lot, so I think it's cheaper and better if you just help me out a little, because I'd love to continue working with you."

"Lastly, let me add, if you do this, I promise to be even more on top of my shit. Better with infields, figuring out better ways to make your life easier. By the way, I'm not giving you an ultimatum, I'm just telling you my situation."

All this time Max is looking at me carefully, and nodding. I can't tell exactly how he felt, because he was in the midst of the whole depression thing. I actually felt even worse for bringing this topic up then, his face was a pale, greenish color, and there were dark circles under his eyes. But it was our last week before the break and I needed to establish that.

I was kinda expecting a long discussion, because I prepared so much for this talk, etc. And then Max looked at me and said:

"That's cool man."
"Yeah, I was actually wanting to cover your flights from now on; I cover Vini's too. You know what, I won't only cover your USA flights, but also the ones we'll do at the start of the next year before Vini joins us again: the Amsterdam and Copenhagen ones."

"And yeah, all the teaching and training somebody new, and the trust issues, I don't wanna do that. And also, as I told you before, I'm really glad to have you on the team. So I'm definitely cool with that."

A warm and fuzzy feeling started to arise in my stomach. I looked Max in the eyes and thanked him, and then went to finish my smoothie. I kept cool, but on the inside I was screaming with joy. I could continue to do something that I love, and I would not have to be broke after.

My hands were shaking. I spent a lot of time and energy preparing for this talk. I discussed my options with a few of my best friends and with part of my family. A lot was at stake. And it went even better than I imagined. I was truly happy.

You see the thing I didn't tell Max, is that I would probably still continue to travel with him, even if I had to be broke after. I was considering getting a loan, and a good friend from London also offered a thousand or two if I ever needed to borrow it.

There is this interesting logic I have about money. I track my expenses, I like to know where I am, and there is always a safety line. For me that is 1000-2000€. I never go below that. I would rather work in a McDonald's than go below that, because being broke sucks. I only had been broke once in my life, and it felt terrible.

Here, I'd probably risk it. Because the value in skill acquisition and networking was so disproportionate. Even fully broke, I could just get some boring job and have that one to two thousand back in a few months. I knew it would stop my progress drastically; once you're in the rat race, it's hard to climb out. You need to be really resourceful to figure it out.

But luckily, I didn't have to worry about that anymore.

So anyway, I was beaming with joy and was super happy. I told my mum, and a few of my best friends. And when I was doing something with Vini later on, he congratulated me.

"So you're getting your flights covered now, huh, bro? Awesome job man, that was pretty smooth."

I thanked him, and said that I was actually preparing the talk like a crazy man, and that I was nervous as hell. He said he could see that, but that I still did an awesome job. I saw a glitter of respect in his eyes.

And it was the "real bro" respect. There was not a sliver of jealousy, but only respect and genuine happiness. Something you feel when someone close to you outdoes themselves. It's motivating, warm, and contagious.

So despite all the darkness and depression, despite being tired and frustrated, I was also happy.

Let the adventures continue.

Chapter Thirteen
THE GOTHENBURG SPEECH THERAPY

Gothenburg Free Tour, December 2015

I arrived at the Airbnb. Everything was dark and grim, the evil energy continued to linger there. I felt like I was in a hospital, but without the bad smell.

So I catch up with Vini (Max is sleeping I think), and we head to the venue. I was really hoping Max wouldn't fall asleep; he had been popping a lot of melatonin (a sleeping supplement) over the last few days.

I actually helped Max get the supplement from my host. It's not as bad as sleeping pills, and it does help with sleep. And of course, it's better to take a sleep supplement and actually get some sleep, than to just go without sleep at all.

Max had massive insomnia at the time. He has that from time to time, but it seemed to get really bad then. It started in Tallinn, and then continued through Helsinki and then in Gothenburg it went from bad to worse. He told Vini and I about it:

"Dude, I couldn't sleep again. I just laid in bed, trying to fall asleep, but nothing happened. I check my watch, 7am, still awake. I think I passed out for an hour around 9, but that's about it. I don't know how I'll get through the day, man, I really need some sleep."

Damn, Max had it pretty rough. I even discussed therapy with him. I mean, his mom is a therapist so he's not prejudiced about that. I had some therapy in my student days too, and it really helped.
If he didn't fix something, it would be a struggle to continue traveling with him.

Anyway, Vini and I arrive early to the hotel where we'll be delivering the Free Tour, meet the volunteers, and arrange everything. It was good to meet the volunteers, they were all young guys, full of energy, happy, accomplished. They were all excited about RSD, about game, and about life. It felt good, I noticed what Max meant when he said that my positivity was contagious. Except that I was on the receiving end now.

Max comes and we are about to start the Free Tour. He doesn't look too good. He has gained some weight lately, to the point where you can see the man boobs showing. And he looks tired, tired as hell. There are dark circles under his eyes and his head-to-toe black outfit seems to reflect his mood.

Usually we'd play a kickass intro, and then he'd run to the stage accompanied by everyone cheering and boosting him up.

This time, no intro.

Vini announces him, tells the gym Tinder story to hype the audience a bit. Vini's normally great at public speaking, but it didn't work so well this time. He got a few laughs, it was a good story, but I guess our energy was just too negative. And then Max emerges from the back. He walks slowly, less energetically than usual, yet, still grounded in a way. He addresses the crowd in an easy, steady voice, sitting on a chair:

"What's up, Gothenburg."

"This World Tour was awesome, I'm really happy about it. We've been killing it, my brand is doing better than ever, and I have a product coming up. I'm very proud of all my students, I had this one guy, who was very distrustful, a big sceptic, yet he pulled every night...

I learned a lot, I grew a lot. I met so many amazing people, some amazing girls. Yet, this is the last city of the tour. The truth is, I am massively overworked and burnt out. I can't sleep lately, I have bad insomnia. I just roll around in the bed for hours, without any sleep. I'm even popping some sleeping supplement pills."

I observe how true Max is to himself, and I respect him for that. He didn't open the crowd with some high energy stories as usual, he didn't make a lot of funny jokes. He kind of dove straight into how things are: he's burnt out and doesn't feel well. He teaches guys to be genuine and true to how they feel at all times, and the teaching is based on himself.

"I lost my appetite too. And you have to understand this, I'm a natural fatty, even when people die in my family, I can still eat.

Lately I don't really feel like eating. If I do manage to eat, it's some crap like Ben & Jerry's or some crisps. It's been weeks since I last meditated, and I've stopped going to the gym.

And then yesterday, at some point, I made a smoothie because I couldn't eat, but knew I needed to get calories in, even though I was not hungry. And I stand there in the kitchen, at the window, and think. I was thinking about all kinds of stuff, but it was pretty dark. And it was getting darker. And then I look down the window and THE thought creeps in:

"What would happen if I just jumped?"

At this point you'd see the guys in the audience start to whisper and look around for a bit, as if they were unsure if this really was RSD Max. They were expecting tips on how to get with hot girls, how to kill it in life and hustle. And here is this guy, talking about his suicidal thoughts...

"And then I was like, whoa, what the fuck was that thought? It scared the hell out of me and it made me think. And it's not that I really considered jumping or anything like that. But the fact that the thought came into my mind somehow was scary. It was like an alarm that tells you to get your shit together.

"I thought for a long while, and at some point I realized that my motivation is completely fucked up. Because I motivate myself from the wrong place. My motivation goes like this:

"Max, if you don't edit this video now, you're a worthless piece of shit." Max, if you don't approach that hottie right now, you're a worthless piece of shit. Max if your product launch is not the biggest seller in RSD history, you're a worthless piece of shit."

"And true, I've accomplished a lot in these last two years. It's crazy. It's beyond crazy. I'm traveling the world, teaching

Bootcamps and seminars, got 60k+ YouTube subscriptions. My brand is growing with an amazing speed..."

I'm changing lives too, and making a really good living at the same time. It's been awesome. But all I'm saying is, there's a price too. And people don't see that when they come up to me to ask for some game advice, or when they admire me so much, and wish they could swap lives with me.

And I finally understood it, that even though I'm killing it in most aspects, my motivation hasn't been right. It came from a wrong place. There was no love in me..."

I watched Max transform there on the stage. It really was like he had this collective psychotherapy going on. Just pouring out things that have been bugging him to the crowd. No masks, no bullshit, just pouring out straight from the deep places that we normally show only to a select few. People were drawn into that. He was so real, so raw, that people listened.

And that's a big thing to say, because the majority of these guys came there to learn how to fuck girls. Instead, they listened for two hours to a guy talking about how tired and sad he is, and how he can't sleep, and how he learned he needs to love himself more. It was in a way totally bizarre and in a way amazing beyond words.

Later on, while me and Vini were packing the gear, I noticed Max seemed a bit better. Still tired, still drained, but it seemed as if the Free Tour speech, sharing and giving from his core, had somehow given him a little more strength. A little bit of the spark returned to his eyes. Hopefully, just enough to get him through the last week of this tour.

After the tour, another amazing thing happened. The selling of the Hot Seat went super well. Max didn't even try to pitch it hard. He just kind of offered the product. And people responded, they bought more than ever, we had an almost 40% sell rate, which is basically unheard of.

And I felt really sorry for him at that point. He finished the speech, seemed a little better, and then needed to head out straight to the Bootcamp venue, to teach guys how to get laid. That's rough, man.

I guess the life of a RSD instructor never seemed that rewarding to me again after witnessing this.

Chapter Fourteen

THE BIRTHDAY THAT SAVED US ALL

There was one really positive thing in Gothenburg that week though. We had a birthday celebration for Vini. I forgot which day of the week it was, but I remember Max had me go to Apple store a few days before in Helsinki to buy the new *BB8* drone from the recent *Star Wars* movie. An expensive (200€) geeky toy, that Max would love to get himself.

He's like a kid regarding those things, haha. For example, I have no doubt that Vini would appreciate it a lot more, if Max told him: *"Listen man, you've been doing really well, here's 200€, Happy Birthday."*

But well, Max being Max, he bought Vini the drone. I mean, the drone was pretty cool to be honest. It could patrol around, you can voice command it, there were even some hologram options. A pretty cool toy indeed. I went to the shop and got two cakes as well, nobody gave two fucks about not eating sugar anymore.

We totally surprised Vini and it was beautiful. His eyes grew big when he received the wrapped box from Max, and after opening it, his mouth became winder and turned into a tired smile too. We sang the birthday song, I brought out the cakes, and I think we even had candles.

That's the only really positive moment that I remember from inside that Airbnb in Gothenburg. The only other was when we were cleaning and packing the last day.

During the celebration, Vini tried his best to be happy, he was obviously very tired and not in a celebration mood. Max was in an even worse state, all grim and pale, dark bags under his eyes, but still really trying to pull the last bits of positivity out of himself for Vini.

It was a comic sight looking back to it. Max, eating ice-cream and trying to smile from behind his computer screen. Vini, with the BB8 drone in his hand figuring out if he has enough energy to scroll through instructions. And myself, initiating the birthday song and candles, trying to be strong and positive so the "family" could feel the same. Three war veterans, completely drained of life, trying to celebrate life, and be happy for a birthday.

But it was good that we did it, maybe that saved us all. It was far from perfect, yet it mattered a lot. We all had some cake, Vini played around with the drone, and I shot a few vids of us celebrating and singing.

That brought a little bit of the Christmas spirit back. We were all torn inside, but we still did our best to hang out and to celebrate together.

I grew up a lot in that week, but the biggest growth was

yet to come.

I've seen where going down the rabbit hole can bring you, but I haven't ventured there myself...

Chapter Fifteen
A DARK FAREWELL

Gothenburg, December 2015

I vividly remember the last day.

We were about to have a three-week New Year's holiday. After that, Max and I would start touring again in January, and then Vini would join a month later in the USA, because he had some problems with his Brazilian Visa.

As always, we pack our bags, and I help the guys clean the flat a bit. Nobody gives too much of a fuck about the flat being super clean, because we were all just too tired. In fact, there was actually a spark of positivity in the air, we were all happy the tour is ending and that we're getting some time off.

I had three more days in Gothenburg, because I'd fly straight to London on Christmas Eve; the flights were cheaper then. My Gothenburg host was awesome, he'd allow me to crash at his place for 10 days in total, that was really epic...

So we left the flat, and the guys were waiting for an Uber. I was always pretty good at goodbyes, but most people suck.

They don't know what to do, and then important things usually stay unsaid, unexpressed. The only proper farewells I had were during the times I was working in children's therapeutic organizations. People there are sensitive, they are in touch with their emotions, they are expressive.

So anyway, Max and Vini kinda sucked with goodbyes too. I'd like it if we could all stand in a circle and share how we feel. If we could tell each other *"I'll miss you!"* and *"Get some rest bro, you need it."* But I don't force this approach down people's throats, usually they don't get it, and that's fine.

We just kinda troll around and say random shit to pass the time, and then the Uber comes. I wish them a pleasant holiday and say that we'll be in touch anyway. The guys say something along the same lines.

The Uber drives off and I look after them. And then just before leaving to my host's, something surprises me. Max and Vini pop out of the windows, their faces, hands and parts of torso pointing out of the car. And they start yelling something along the lines of:

"Bostjaaaaannn, mmmm, ach yaaaa..." in the weird, funny, German porn voice. We would always imitate the really bad, old school German porn actors, and shout random phrases in "dirty" German to make them sound really funny.

It was super weird to an outsider, but it felt really good to me. We were good friends, we'd been on a roller-coaster ride than some friendships have not seen in the course of a lifetime, and we would not see each other for a while.

Let the holidays begin.

Chapter Sixteen

ON FEMININE ENERGY AND SLUT SHAMING

London, December 2015

I landed in London, got the keys to my place, and then headed to London Liverpool St. Station, where I was about to meet this cool Latina girl. She's from Chile, lives in Barcelona, I met her in Paris, and now she came to visit me in London.

There's a long backstory that ranges from one of the most romantic and sexy nights with her in Paris, to a lot of drama, crying and bullshit when I visited her in Barcelona. I guess round 3 will be in London, haha.

I'm super happy to see her when she comes. She's a very stylish girl, so she's dressed nice. Her tiger-patterned handbag stands out from her designer coat and tight black leggings and a black bonnet. We hug each other, and based on the hug, she's down again. I guess all the drama from Barcelona evaporated a bit, and we were both in a better mindset.

I'd like to mention that I was really grounded and had a solid state from all the travels – not many things could rock my boat. But, I was also tired as hell. We take an Uber back to where I was staying - I had a volunteer give me his room for three weeks in exchange for some coaching later on. In the Uber we kiss, and it's super on again.

We get to the flat, and I obviously wanted to have sex. We drop her bags, I show her around, take her to the room and start to kiss her. She's not really down for that, she wants to go visit tourist attractions. And that kind of set the tone for the next few days.

It was confusing me, she would be super down at some points, and super off at others. We would be passionately kissing each other, dry-humping, I would be rubbing her pussy. She'd touch my dick, she'd moan hard and I could feel how wet she was. But we'd never end up having sex.

I showed her around London, we cuddled, I'd make her feel very special, we'd cook together. And then the above story would repeat itself. No matter what happened, she was not down to have sex. And that was really frustrating. I mean, I jerked off to her, she even helped a little, but it was just not the same.

The thing is, she was super, super horny, but the social conditioning would slut shame her and once it got "too serious" she would panic and block out her sexuality. I guess it had something to do with her being raised in a very conservative household. Oh, she was still a virgin at 21. I guess that played a big role too.

I fucking hate slut-shaming and societal pressure. Wouldn't the world be kinder and nicer if two people that like each other could just have sex without some pressure or judging? We clearly liked each other, and were super attracted. It would just be such an upgrade of our shared experience, but because of some conservative beliefs, it ended in frustration instead.

Gets me frustrated every time.

The next thing I learned from her is that her kind of feminine energy is really chaotic.

Let me explain.

She almost left at some point. I had to run after her one time, when she stormed off with her bags. I apologized, told her that I didn't want her to go. I saw she was on the brink of crying and I felt really bad. In fact, I felt so bad I had teary eyes myself. I was being a bit of a dick too.

And you know what the cause of this fight was? She wanted to go out, and have a drink while I wanted to eat first.

Let me explain.

I refused, I said that I first want to eat, and then go out and have a drink. Something really stupid, right? But you see, this is one way of how some women test men. Can I hold my own, or will I cater to all of her desires as soon as she mentions them?

If I failed that test, she'd lose respect for me as a man. I'd be just another spineless loser, who will submit to her, simply because she's a hot girl. It doesn't work like that.

This is quite abstract, so let me give an example of a small child. A child will often test the limits with parents. And some parents are really bad at establishing boundaries. The child will always get their own way and it's not good for them.

In this case, she didn't really care about the drink right then. She was testing my masculinity. Was I just another one of those men who would let her go her way just because she's a pretty girl, not daring to displease her? Or was I somebody who could "handle" her?

By the way, just to make it clear, I'm not saying "be a dick to girls" here. It doesn't mean that if your girl has a better idea, you always have to go with your own. I'm just saying that you don't have to comply with every little whim the girl has. On the contrary, sometimes she will, subconsciously, test you for your masculinity like this.

And once you maintain your own, it shows her that you are stable, and no matter how much she rocks your boat, you will not turn over. A lot of girls are emotionally scattered all around, most of the time. From laughing to crying to screaming in minutes. So once they meet a man that can help them be more grounded, they really hook hard.

The reward I'd get for that is her femininity. She'd cook for me; the guacamole she'd make for me was AMAZING. We had an amazing Christmas dinner, I even invited my dad, and we had a lovely time. She'd massage me, caress me, and kiss me passionately.

She'd sing in her beautiful voice to her favorite songs out

loud. Do you know how rare it is for guys to sing along to songs? So hearing a girl singing to some girly song is just awesome, it's goofy, it's warm, it's really cool.

It was beautiful.

However, we had this pattern repeat itself a lot during the five days. We'd have an awesome cuddling time, passionate make out sessions full of grabbing, dry humping, and jerking off. And then we'd have a lot of fights too. She'd withdraw, I would leave her alone for some time. Then one of us would come back to the other and another cycle began.

It was really intense, I felt a lot of different emotions, I get why some couples get hooked on this. But I don't think it's really healthy. Too much emotional drama for me.

And I arrived at the conclusion that the more feminine the girl is, the more chaotic she will be, and the more she will test you. But on the other hand of the testing, if you pass it, are the amazing vibes, warmth, the girliness, and passion.

So these go hand in hand, which is okay.

It didn't end too well, however. She was content with playing around, but I still wanted to have sex. I guess I pushed for it a little too much. Last night we kind of slept on the far sides of the bed, and broke contact after a few days. I noticed she unfriended me on Facebook.

Oh well.

Chapter Seventeen

HOW LONDON SAVED MY LIFE - LOVE 2.0

London, December 2015

So after the Chilean girl left, I still had about two weeks in London before I would visit Slovenia for a week and afterwards continue the tour. I hadn't gotten laid for some time, and all the tiredness started to come back.

I was not really going out that much. I couldn't be bothered, to be honest, since I didn't really want to run around in clubs after the last few months. I was working a little bit on my website, my brand, but other than that, I just chilled a lot too. I had to run a Bootcamp for my host and a friend later on, but that was about it with the gaming commitments.

Luckily, Alex was returning from her Christmas holiday back in the Czech Republic. So I met up with her, and the

2nd "honeymoon" period started. It was awesome. I would meet her in our park, we'd go buy some groceries, go back to my place, fuck, then cook an awesome meal, and then fuck. And then cuddle, watch YouTube, chill, and fuck again.

It was so awesome, and so restorative. I really needed that feminine energy, I craved it. Not just the sex. Well, that too, but the whole package really. The cuddling, caressing her cheek, passionate kissing, feeling the warmth of her body next to me, the look in her eyes when I penetrated her. It was awesome, kind of like a boyfriend-girlfriend thing, but better.

I even took her out a few times. Once, I took her to my favorite place to go out to in London – one of the biggest gay clubs in Europe. They did straight nights on Mondays, so I told her to dress up sexy, and off we went. It's an awesome venue, very crazy, very open-minded, a lot of different dance floors, music selections, smoking areas, etc.

I'd show her around, observe the vibe of the club with her. Dance sexy and really close with her, make out passionately. And boy, was she sexy that night. I remember her vividly, she wore black sneakers and tight black leggings. Her top was black satin, semi-transparent, so you could clearly see the shape of her bra and her beautiful boobs. Her back was completely bare, except for a few straps that held the top together.

Oh my god, when I saw her like that, I could barely keep myself from ripping the clothes off of her straight away. And she sensed that from the look in my eyes, and she loved it. I felt that when she danced with me, I felt how she pressed herself against me, how she touched me. She wanted me as badly as I wanted her, and me showing very openly how I feel about her was a major turn on.

And I wasn't the only one who noticed her. I could feel the guys and the girls eyeing her constantly. At some point I popped to the toilet, and when I came back I saw a guy hitting on her. But I was cool with it, I let them chat for some time. She was hot, and there's nothing wrong if she has a bit of a banter with some guy. Then I entered the set, the guy saw what was up, and after some time fist-bumped me and left.

Out in the smoking area, we chat up some people. We even chatted up some girls together. Before that I asked if she ever wanted to have a threesome, and she was pretty open about it. Not like full on, but pretty open to the idea.

I remember this blonde that I opened, she was all over me in a second. I introduce Alex to her as my cousin. And then after a few mins of chatting, I just make out hardcore with Alex. The blonde goes like, *"omg, what the fuck."* But really, she loved it. She loved us, my girl, me. She was super touchy with me.

So at some point I brought her closer in, and we all had a short three-way kiss. However, I sensed Alex was not 100% comfortable with this, so I didn't really push it further. No problem, it was our night, and that was just extra fun. But I still thought it was super cool that she was not judgmental and was open to situations like that.

Many months later on, after the whole world traveling adventure, when I visited her in London, I saw the wristband from the club in her room. It really warmed my heart to see that. I loved that she had kept a souvenir from that amazing experience we shared together.

You see, the thing about this girl was, she was super cool and laid back. She wouldn't mind when we ate some cheap food. She was cool when we had to sit outside. She would love to be fucked fiercely. She'd caress me when I needed that. And never, ever, would she try to make me feel bad, or play the jealousy card.

She knew I met other girls, but never mentioned that I shouldn't go out, or anything like that. She gently teased me at some points later on: *"How was the competition in Miami?"* but no more than that. I liked that about her, she would never try to pressure me.

And slowly but steadily, I started to fall in love with her.

You see, I had met a lot of girls in the recent months, and I noticed she had a lot going for her. A lot that I would search for in a girl. She was really hot and sexy. She was kinky, open minded. Also very pragmatic and simple. She was a hard worker, very brave, and great with kids, which I appreciate a lot. Just a very good combination of personality traits in a girl.

I even took her to the tallest building in London, a somewhat posh and fancy venue. She dressed up super nice (she didn't want to wear high heels though, because she'd be taller than me that way, haha). I put on my blazer, some nice shoes, and off we went.

Now, I bought us the cheapest drinks there, the honey beer, which was I think about £6 per bottle. But it was still awesome. And again, she'd not complain about not having a £20 cocktail, and I know a lot of girls that would. She'd instead appreciate the experience. Great view, dim lights, awesome company, the passion in our eyes.

It's not something you'd do all the time, but it was nice from time to time. And me being crazy, and her being such a great girl, something really exciting happened too. When we were done with our beers, we leave towards the exit. A kinky idea creeps up into my mind:

"Let's go to the toilet first."

We go to the toilet - and even the toilets up in that skyscraper are kinda nice, awesome view, etc. I quickly checked that there was nobody in the male toilet, and then just dragged her into the cubicle with me. I pushed her to the wall and kissed her. She was just so hot in that dress, showing off a nice part of her boobs and I could see the shape of her beautiful ass.

"Mmm, baby, I want you to suck my dick now."

Her eyes were on fire, I knew she was totally turned on. She really loved dirty talking. She starts to suck my dick and it gets me really hard, really fast. It was still kind of a mind fuck. I was at this awesome posh venue, with a beautiful girl, and she was blowing me in the toilet. Who would have ever thought, haha.

Then I push her to the wall again, pull her hair, and kiss her neck.

"Yeah, you like me pulling your hair, don't you? You like sucking my dick in this fancy toilet, huh? I bet you really want me to fuck you right now..."

"Oh, yes, come on, fuck me already!"

And then I turn her around, bend her over, pull her fancy dress higher and her stockings lower and fuck her right there in the toilet on the 50th floor, overseeing the magical London. It ends pretty fast, since I was actually slightly nervous, but didn't want to show it.

A slightly embarrassing thing happened too, as she blew me in the end. Some cum fell onto my nice trouser pants, so I kind of had to hide that by holding my blazer in my hands so it covered the massive cum-stain.

Kinky smiles on both of our faces, we left.

Chapter Eighteen
"CUZ THE PLAYER'S GONNA PLAY, PLAY, PLAY..."

London, January 2016

I didn't see Alex every day though, and that was good. I think some couples have problems because they just stick together too much. They spend every single minute of every single day together, and they obviously become bored.

You need to spice it up a bit, so that the time you do spend together is amazing, and you give your everything to the other person. Anyway, me being a player, and me going out for the Bootcamp I was giving to the guys, I met some other girls too. And one of them in particular, an Italian girl, was really down. Even her girlfriend told me, *"Dude, she wants to kiss you..."*

So I made out with her in the pub that night, got her

number, and left it at that.

I met that Italian girl on one of the days I wasn't with Alex. I met her at the tube station close to my place, took her to the grocery store, and talked about how much I like avocados. Just something to rumble about so there was no "uncomfortable silence."

Told her we'll skip the "super cool coffee place" that I wanted to take her to, because I was sitting around having coffees all day. Instead, I took her straight to mine. There we chat for a bit, I show her some videos, we play some music. She gives me a little shit while we are getting very touchy with each other:

"Do you do this with every girl?"

"Of course, you are number 47 today..."

Just a little shit from her side, to see how I will react. And when it didn't bother me too much, it was all good and we continued. Just before sex, a little more testing came out:

"I should be going now..."

"That's okay baby, you can leave when you need to..."

I just brush everything off, and half an hour later, she is sucking my dick. The sex was pretty good, and she gave nice blowjobs. We fuck two more times, and then she leaves. I teased her in the end:

"I thought you had to leave early."

The reason I'm mentioning this is to explain that I was still in love with Alex.

I don't know if this makes any sense, but I liked pimping it, I liked the challenge, the chase and being chased. I liked the excitement of having sex with a new girl. But I'd never take that girl over my girl.

And when I met Alex, I'd be amazing to her. I'd take her to nice places, make her feel special, fuck her like she wanted it. Give my all and my best to her.

So it's a really funny thing, love. Makes us do heroic deeds, and crazy shit. Two sides of the same coin. And monogamy, well, to be honest, I don't know if that works.

But let's not go into that now.

Chapter Nineteen
KEEPING IN TOUCH

London, January 2016

*"RSD Maximilian invited you to a play a game of "Command &
Conquer Zero Hour Generals" with him. Do you want to accept
the invitation?"*

"The invitation has been accepted."

I was still doing a bit of work for Max during the break,
but not too much. We agreed I'll finish two very long
censoring clips, but in the end I only did one. I needed
some time off too, and I was working on my emerging
brand too, the YouTube channel called BossLifeHacks,
together with the BossLifeHacks.com website.

Yet, Max and I kind of got hooked on C & C, so we had a
few sessions where we'd play.

"Hey bro, how's Austria, are you getting some rest?"

*"Yeah man, it's so good man, no traveling. I'm just getting high,
overeating, and jerking off all day, I really needed this. I'm about*

to start some therapy too, so I'm looking forward to that."

"Yeah bro, you were pretty burnt out back in Gothenburg huh?"

"Dude, it's not even funny, it's been crazy. I'm still feeling like shit, but it's slowly getting better. To be honest, it sounds funny, but all the weed and jerking off helps. I'm also at a super nice place. I'm in my mom's flat here in Austria. It's beautiful, man. Snow everywhere around me, a giant lake, mountains. The nature is crazy beautiful here man. It feels good."

"Awesome man, I'm super happy for you. Btw, listen, the censoring, it's not going that quickly. But I'm hanging with my Czech girl a lot. I mean, I really like her, it's crazy. Think I'm falling in love, lol."

"No worries man, you need some time off too, don't stress too much, even if you don't finish it. And enjoy the time with your girl, you deserved it! Anyway, ready to get your ass kicked in C&C, bro?"

And so we play a few games. There's a lot of Humvees and Comanchee Helicopters and Scorpion Tanks and Elite Hackers and Black Lotus Spies. And all kinds of other warfare stuff. I blast *The Prodigy* through my headphones and just game with Max for an hour or two, it feels good, even though I lose most of the time. Even when gaming, Max was still incredibly on top of his shit and very competitive.

It's funny, because even though we were on a break, we still kind of stayed in touch via the computer game. It was a lot about playing and letting some steam out, but it was also about those few lines of *"how are you,"* etc. That was good. We went through a lot, so it was easier to understand each other.

Somebody who didn't go through the tour wouldn't get it. They would not understand that there comes a time where you just don't want or need to do shit. Nothing else except smoking weed, playing games, and jerking off.

And that's fine.

Chapter Twenty

I RUN MY FIRST BOOTCAMP

London, January 2016

Damn. That blonde was super hot. A Swedish girl, 20 years old, with super tight body. She was slightly drunk, out on a Thursday evening on her last night in London. No shit, she was down to have sex that night.

However, the student always has the priority. And then instead of hot sex with this super hot blonde, I watched how the student "ruined" the set. And then I masturbated at home. Damn, I know how Max feels at times now.

It all began a few hours ago, when I met my two students at the local casino on Leicester Square. It's a good meeting (or date) spot, nice and comfy, open all night, clean toilets. Hell, you even get free drinks in most casinos.

It was my first time running a Bootcamp. Unofficially, of course. I also didn't charge for it. One student was a good friend who actually persuaded me to become an assistant, so I wanted to give him something in return, and the other was the guy who had given me his room in London for the fourteen days.

The last part of the crew was Pete, a guy who I knew from my earlier pimping days in London. He had sick game, pulled both times when I went out with him, and he had coached at Vegas Immersion, another RSD program, for some time. I have a lot of respect for this guy.

So the two guys roll in, me and Pete are already waiting. I do the bro handshake for my friend Ward and introduce myself to Rish. They were both normal, late 20s, decent sense of fashion, and not socially super awkward. Cool, no hard-case newbies.

We head straight to the club, since it's already close to 11pm. I don't want to risk us not getting in due to cues. We get in easily, helped by my strict requests to be smartly dressed. I sit them down at the table and give them an outline of the weekend. Basically, more or less all the stuff I learned from Max:

"Hey guys, by now you know me, I'm Bostjan, and I've been gaming for about 6 years now. The last 3 months, I was traveling around the world with RSD Max, THE fastest-growing game coach right now. We've had Bootcamps and the Hot Seat almost every single weekend for the past 3 months. Trust me when I say this, I've seen it all.

All the sticking points, all the excuses, all the fixes. Trust me, if you do what I say, you will progress in the game. My role here is to push you out of your comfort zone, to give you feedback, and to inspire you, so you'll see me in action too.

Now, you have to know some things too. This is not a Thailand Sex tour, the goal here is not "just" to get laid. Okay, if it happens, cool. But the goal is to teach you how to be self-sufficient. In three days I wont be here to push you anymore, so you better learn how to do this for yourself..."

After the briefing, we went straight to action. I point some girls out to the guys and they go and open them.

Rish is too aggressive, he doesn't have a lot of fear, but struggles to stay in set with the girl for longer. Also, he has massive filters and uses a lot of bullshit ideas he had previously "learned" from some other pickup and dating companies. Things like scripted lines, routines, etc. Things that might work initially, but once you want to actually connect and share with the girl, it backfires.

Ward is a bit more experienced, but also more stifled. He tries too hard to "just make the girl like him." He also gets easily discouraged after a rejection and takes it very personally. He's a super cool and funny guy, he's smart, makes a lot of money, but there's a deep sense of "not being enough" in him. Like so many other guys, even me, in the field.

So towards the end of the first night we end up on the same table. Two chicks, Rish, me, and Ward. Pete is in set with the third girl of our two-girl set somewhere else. Ward is doing phenomenally, and after a bit of my help via texting, he moves closer to his girl, vibes, and later on makes out with her.

Rish is trying to get the blonde attracted. However, it's backfiring as it usually does when you try too hard. And again, as it usually happens, she instead focuses on the guy who didn't give a shit: in this case, me.

So while she's asking me questions and being touchy feely with me, Rish is trying desperately to get her attention back. Because I know he likes her, I don't really interact with her, which in turn makes her even more attracted. Weird logic, but some girls actually think like this:

"Why doesn't that guy give a shit about me, I'm super hot... I'll MAKE him notice me..."

And it was my mistake to be honest; she was hot, I did want her, and she clearly wanted me. However, I didn't want to be a dick to Rish. The guy gave me his own room for two weeks, and that's worth a lot of money if you are living in London. Also, it was the first time we've met.

Fuck my life.

Flash forward half an hour, the set fizzles. Pete came back without his girl, his set had burned out because he had put on too much pressure to pull. The blonde got too drunk to be pulled anyway, and Ward somehow signaled that even though he had made out with the other girl, he now preferred the blonde.

The blonde, who didn't like Rish, and who I was leaving alone so I could be a "good teacher," was by now, really wasted and pretty much a mess, haha. But the game is like this most of the time. It's not clear, it's messy. Which makes it fun and challenging.

We all do a few more sets, and I head home at 2.30am. Ward is pretty happy, Rish is not very impressed, and Pete stays and roams the streets because he really wants to get laid. We schedule a meet up the next night at a different, more high class venue.

Next Evening

We meet at the nearby McDonalds, the guys are a bit late and I get angry. I tell them off, showing how I am giving them a lot of value (The official RSD Bootcamp costs thousands of dollars) and they've shit on it. After my outburst, I go through their sticking points and what we need to work on.

"Okay Rish, look, you're good with opening, there's no fear in you, that's really, really good. However, you're a big guy, and you can seem intimidating to a girl. So smile a bit when you first open, it makes you a lot less threatening. Also, we'll work on you just staying in the set, vibing, talking about stuff.

Look, you don't need to say something super amazing and really clever. Instead, chill. Just talk about anything, as if chatting to a mate. Talk about what you like, talk about what you hate. You two are, after all, trying to get to know each other. At the same time, monitor her. If it gets boring, you can bust out a joke or two, or some teasing..."

Some girls overhear our conversation, or better said, me repeating strategies I learned from the time with Max, and get a bit offended. After a while, they verbally attack me directly:

"Don't listen to this guy, he doesn't know shit and you guys are better off not listening to his advice."

To be honest, getting girl advice from a girl rarely works. Sometimes it does, but mostly a girl will just tell you something like: *"Just be yourself."*

Well, thanks, that helps. But, how do I do that? Or they'll

tell you something like: *"Relax, act natural, and just go and tell her you like her, offer to buy her a drink."*

And then 10min later, after buying the drink, the girl is like: *"Okay, thanks for the drink, you have a great night buddy..."*

Anyway, I mostly ignore the girls and continue the discussion, I couldn't be bothered to try to explain anything to them. They try even harder to get my attention and after some time I tell them off in a very cocky manner:

"Look, ladies, we're talking about something important here and you weren't invited. If you want we can chat about it later on in the club, I think we're going to the same venue."

"Hah, forget about it!"

After saying that, they open the door and leave. And just before that, one of them gives me the finger too. The situation is super tense and half of the restaurant is looking at us.

I call after her with a big grin:

"Call me later, darling!"

We all laugh about it, and the atmosphere relaxes. In fact, even the guy cleaning the tables gets a big smile on his face. The two students were a bit tense from the argument, but are soon back to normal when I positively color the situation.

"Look, this is the same as game. They were just giving us some shit. They don't know us. They don't know we all work hard at improving our lives. They don't know we will probably be the

only sober guys in the club trying to meet some girls.

She was just pissed at the persona she constructed in her head of me. She thought I was some loser who's giving loser advice to his loser friends. That doesn't make me one. The mistake most guys make, is that they fall into that trap. She sees you like that, and you just start to act like that then. No, fuck that.

You are who you are, you are a cool-ass fucking dude, trying to make a beautiful connection happen, and if she's too narrow-minded to see through that, why bother? Fuck it, just smile, tell her she's gorgeous, and move on."

We head to the club. My first time there actually. Pete proves his worth, he knows all the staff, gets us in for free, easily. That was smooth. It's a very nice place, beautifully lit gardens on a rooftop terrace, a live DJ, great atmosphere. Although a bit cold in January.

It was a very good night for all of us. I had some amazing sets. An older girl totally wanted to do me, but it was too early, plus I had the students there. Then a super hot girl in very revealing clothes came close to our group. I casually opened her in front of all of her friends, made friends with them all, and then switched to chatting her up.

She was openly flirting with me, but I sensed that she was just trying to make her boyfriend jealous. I also met a girl who I saved into my phone as "potential soulmate" at the end of the night. You know, when you keep staring into each other's eyes for eternity and all time stops. Really cool girl, into same stuff as me, artsy, etc...

I tried to kiss her at some point, but was slightly uncalibrated. We exchanged numbers, but I was sadly never able to meet her.

The students did an amazing job too. Rish opened a group with a funny *"How to Masturbate"* YouTube video. It was some funny looking girl with an enormous cucumber in her hands doing weird sounds. They loved him for it, it was the most fun they, and he, had all night.

It completely destroyed his limiting belief about game not being fun, needing scripted lines, etc. He understood that he can just relax a little more. Going out and pimping it is about having some fun with your friends. It's THE time to let go of all the work and other stress and just chill and troll around for a bit. Everybody's more open to jokes as they are out to have fun too.

I helped Ward fix a major sticking point, which was talking too much and not making any pauses with eye contact.

You see, a pause gives the girl a chance to start talking herself, you don't want to have monologues all night. Sometimes it's great to just shut up, look deep into her eyes, and listen. And in those seconds, before she says something, you guys can have a few moments of connection without words, which is way more powerful.

After he introduced some well-timed pauses, the girls would be way more hooked into interactions. He couldn't even believe that a small tweak like this would improve his interactions so much. The girls started to open up to him way more and he could just relax and absorb some of their energy instead of just thinking about which joke to bust out next.

At some point we were even in a set together, and I was hitting on a girl, that soon turned to Ward, because he was such a boss. I was trying a bit too hard there, and he was keeping it chill, and cool, and not talking too much, and so she decided she liked him better. Awesome, I was so happy for him.

I tried to pull the "soulmate" when the club closed, but failed. Not enough comfort with her friends, so I took a night bus ride home with Rish and a few other friends. It reminded me on countless solo night bus rides home from back when I lived in London. Ward stayed with Pete, they were in a set with a bunch of hot Asians.

Somewhere along the way back, about 10 girls entered the bus. After a while I went and sat with them and gave them the best ride of their lives. We joked, took selfies and sang. They totally loved me and the guys watched me with disbelief. Who the hell was this guy who could open a group of 10 girls and make them all love him?

Again, no pull. Looking back, with even some more balls, it could have been possible. Before I go to sleep I receive a text that Ward and Pete are pulling a group of Asians.

Sweet!

Next Afternoon

The next day we meet for the final Bootcamp session in a shopping mall for some day game.

Again, the guys learned a lot. I showed them how day game is actually very similar and how it can be super fun as well. After the session, we had some pizza and covered their sticking points again and made a good game plan for the future.

"Alright guys, as you know, momentum is key here. Like really,

if you want to become good at this, you need to be going out and opening girls, sorry to say, but there's no other way. But on the other hand, you have good momentum now, so use it. Also, go out together, meet more wings, this will help you.

Now you know the sticking points, right? Ward, keep working on silences and just establishing the mindset that you are a really cool guy and girls can be happy to talk to you. And Rish, a little slower sometimes, give the girl a chance to get to know you first, and also, relax, it's fine to do goofy stuff and it doesn't have to be so serious.

Also, guys, feel free to contact me via email at any point. I'll help you out. This has been a really fun experience for me, so thanks guys, I learned a lot, and I hope you did too..."

Before parting, Ward pulled me to the side and surprised me. He pulls out £200 from his pocket and says that the value I gave him was so big, he couldn't let me do it for free, and if I could please accept this small token of appreciation.

DUDEEE, that was so fucking cool. Obviously I was not doing it for the money, but getting that felt like a really nice and well-deserved reward. I did give my 100% to the guys, and I think they got a lot out of it. It also made my stay in London less expensive than anticipated.

And for the first time I started to dream about doing real Bootcamps as an RSD instructor.

Chapter Twenty-One
A HEARTBREAKING EMBRACE

Then New Year's happened, which is another example of how much I've fallen for Alex.

In the evening I chilled with my dad and a wing. We had an awesome, beautiful time. We actually experienced the new year on the tube, the London underground. Like the actual midnight, 00:00, on the tube, in the train. It was funny, we brought champagne and toasted with the other people on the train, even met two cute Hungarian girls.

And then after, we walked around central London, where my buddy Sam was opening girls left and right, and me and my dad chatted. At some point, I tell my dad that it has been really good hanging out with him, but if he sees me chatting up a girl, and I'm with her for more than five minutes, I'm going to try to go with her and I'll catch him later. He gives me a funny look, but agrees. I think he was a bit of a player when he was younger too.

At some point I see a cute two-set, I open and they both hook instantly. Sam joins in, and they like him too. The girls were Dutch tourists, it was their last night in London, and they had awesome logistics, meaning they lived in a hostel with a private room, not far from where we were.

An easy pull.

We walk with them towards the casino, and who do I see? Alex with her girlfriend! Me and Sam are walking hand in hands with the Dutch girls and I make eye contact with Alex. We passed each other. What were the odds?

I freak out a little in my head, then pull myself together, and after about two seconds of thinking finally run to Alex and give her a big bear hug. I decided to just ditch the two-set and join my girl. It was a little shame, because that two-set was super down, and the girls were pretty hot too. But I'd always take my girl over any other.

I felt bad for Sam, because I kind of bailed on him too, and he later on told me he didn't end up pulling the 2 girls. Well, fuck it.

Alex, her girlfriend and I had a really cool New Year's. We walked around central London, I took the girls to the casino, and then to another venue. I totally saved their night too, because all the places were packed full and they didn't have a clue where to go before meeting me.

I even got her friend to love me, that's how much I liked Alex...

So slowly but steadily our time together came to an end. A few days before I left, I needed to move from my beautiful room, because Rish came back. I crashed at my friend

Theodore's for two more nights. On the last night, Alex came over.

We did our favorite combination: cooking and having sex. And then we just cuddled in the living room on the sofa. My flight was at 4am, so we kinda half-napped, half-cuddled through the night. When it was time to go, a strong passion engulfed me.

I felt a strong cocktail of emotions, being sad to leave her, seeing how beautiful she is, loving her, being excited to go on the road again, more sadness. And all those emotions started to turn into one single emotion, passion. Every touch was like fire, and our bodies became one.

I fucked her once more, right there on the sofa with a passion never experienced before. I was penetrating her with long, deep thrusts, as we were kissing each other like there was no tomorrow. Her body was burning, her moans were load, and her fingernails left deep scratches in my back. It was quick and intense, like we would never see each other again.

And then we sat and hugged there, a bundle of arms and legs and hair, naked and sweaty on the sofa, and she wouldn't let me go. I had to leave in 15 minutes, get dressed and all, but she hugged me so tight I could not move. It was as if the breaking of that embrace would break her too.

At that moment, I knew that she didn't just have my heart, I had hers too. And it was fucking difficult to break that embrace. It's hard to describe, but it feels similar to how it must feel when a part of you gets cut off. Literally, when I broke that hug I felt as if I killed a part of myself, as if something was missing. There was a hot, numbing pain in my chest, and an urge in my heart to close the gap and go back into the embrace.

I got dressed, hugged her tightly, and looked her in her teary eyes. She wouldn't cry though, she held it back, she was always very strong like that. Then I pushed her to the wall, passionately kissed her, and then promised I'll see her soon and that I'll stay in touch.

I left without looking back, I didn't want her to see I was crying too.

Chapter Twenty-Two
SEX GOD MODE -
ONE DAY, TWO LAYS

Facebook Inner Circle Slovenia

Double Lay Report

The Afternoon

After London, I had about 10 days back in Slovenia to visit my friends and family, relax a little, and then continue the tour in Europe and USA.

London really had a healing effect on me. My energies were charged and my game was on a crazy level, so I more or less went on a rampage. Anyway, I arrived on Tuesday, Tindered a bit, and matched with a girl who I had tried to get with years before.

She was always like "I can't do this, bla bla..." while at the same time giving signals she did want it. She's not super hot, but she's super cool and fun. So yeah, honestly, I've never had a lay from Tinder before so I just went with it. I text with her a bit, turns out she's "busy," so I take a step back.

"Oh, okay, if you don't wanna meet, that's cool."

And suddenly she's down to meet, haha. I meet her 2pm the following Thursday, I take her straight to the grocery shop next to my place. Grocery shops have become my preferred date location around that time, another golden nugget from Max.

She helps me buy food and then I take her to my place. On the way I see her giving me the Bambi eyes, and I think to myself that she is super down. I put stuff in the fridge, she makes coffee and quite soon, I am standing behind her and kissing her neck. She says:

"We've been here once before, haven't we?"

"Really?"

And I keep going.

We proceed to make out, and after a few minutes I am touching her pussy and she is starting to moan. I thought I went a little too fast, it hasn't even been an hour since I met her. As speculated, she says:

"No, I can't, I'm sorry."

"You're right."

I guess it's time for a takeaway.

I leave her, go sit at the table, open my Mac, and start to ramble on about my next blog article. How, I'm happy with it, what I'll do to improve it, and how many people I expect to read it. I could see her go "what the fuck" in her head. Just one moment ago I was making her super wet and horny, and now here I am, totally cold, talking about some blog article.

After five minutes, I stand up, take her hand, take her to my room without words and proceed to have sex with her. She was really into it this time, and I think she hadn't had sex for a while. She was also on the last days of her period, and luckily, my towel was red so I just put that under us. Felt like such a boy scout, haha.

All this was finished in about two-three hours, then we take the bus together, and I go practice breakdance with my old crew. I return home at 10pm, I'm super fucking tired, take a nap, and wake up at 11.20pm. I quickly cook some tuna pasta,and then hit the centre with my host.

The Evening

There's another big bunch of players meeting us, I guess everyone was excited because RSD Max's assistant, who also happens to be a Slovenian, was in town. We need some time before we decide where to go. First place is quite shitty. But still, I begin by opening up some hotties.

It was crazy, I had some serious killer instinct going on. I was almost like a robot, zero fear, perfectly-timed jokes, zero filters, lazy smile on my face. It almost feels like a cheat code, I've never had such a level of game, and sheer confidence around women before.

I see a mixed three-set: two girls, one guy. I go in with my host and just for fun, push him in and open with:

"Hi, we met on Tinder, do we look cute together?"

Then we just each talk to our girl, and the dude who was originally with the girls chodes out. He has no idea what to do and kinda just stands there while we chat up the girls. These girls are not out for a long time this night, so bad logistics right there. We Facebook-close and move to a different venue. You should see the look on the guy's face. He was helpless. I kinda felt bad for him, because I could relate. But not bad enough to not steal his girls, haha.

I open a few groups on the dance floor with my standard opener, walk straight through the middle of the group to the girl I like, smile, look in her eye and high-five her. "Hi." Works almost every time, they get wet from the confidence and the eye contact.

However, it's a downhill ride after that. We just continue roaming the club, and not much happens. There's a lot of interactions, some funny, some boring, some hot, some not. A beautiful mix of mayhem that is game, the mix I start to love and almost get addicted to.

I open a two-set in the corner, a Lithuanian girl and a Danish girl, both very cute. The Lithuanian instantly grabbed my attention. I have a soft spot for Lithuanian girls - I lived there (Kaunas) for about 10 months. Also, I learned that they have super hot bodies, but sometimes dress weirdly so as not to show it. This seems to be the case again. She had this funny looking sweater, but I could picture a pair of amazing breasts under that.

Anyway, we chat, they love me, but I'm starting to sense the Lithuanian is a bit shy. My buddy comes in, tries to talk to the blonde, but they kind of blow him out out - he was trying way too hard to be funny. I stay in set, just continue to chill and chat. I see the blonde is pretty down for some action tonight.

They say: "Ok, we're going to the dance floor." Most guys fuck it up here, because they just leave them. Instead, I let them know:

"Ok, I'll join you." They're very happy about it. Some French dude starts to dance with the Lithuanian. I'm cool with that, as now I can start to talk to the blonde.

As I get to know her, I see that she's actually really cool. She goes to the gym, she's smart, and a big bonus for me, she smokes weed. The girls need to go to the toilet, but I don't want to wait for them, so I number-close the blonde and say bye-bye.

It was a super solid close too, we made future plans for smoking weed, she gave a lot of Bambi eyes too. I actually told her that I had already gotten laid from Tinder earlier that day. I laughed in my head when this came out of my mouth, haha:

"Don't worry, we can just chill and chat, I'm totally not horny, because I already got laid off of Tinder earlier today."

She tells me I'm a super cool guy and to make sure I call her later. And then they leave.

Next set is some super hot Italian girl.

That was sick actually, they dance on some sort of a stage, two Italian hotties, bellies showing, everyone in the club looking at them, but no guy has the balls to approach. I'm under them, and just poke the hotter of the two through the fence:

"Hey, gimme a high-five."

She doesn't give me the high-five, but smiles and starts to dance a bit more lively.

I continue to talk to her anyway, and she opens rather quickly, after only a minute or two of me still talking to her, even though she had pretended she *"wasn't interested"* at first. Anyway, we chat and after a while the set fizzles. I open some more sets. I'm on fire that night, but I'm getting slightly tired, I had a long day...

Then somehow, I bump into the Lithuanian/Danish two-set again.

"I'm going for some water, come join." They happily come.

A thought pops into my head. It's so funny how most guys are chodes, it makes gaming super easy, because you don't really have to do much. As soon as you even open, and they see you're not shit-faced drunk, you are above 95% of other dudes. And then I realized that I used to be one of the chodes, and I used to have no idea of how the hell to start a conversation with a girl.

And a deep sense of gratitude and growth came to me at that time, and I actually realized that my game had gotten pretty sick.

Anyway, we drink water, chat, and the blonde starts to hit on me hard.

What I mean by that is, she was trying to impress me by telling me how much she hits the gym and how she'll become a lawyer and all that. At the same time, she was looking at my lips ALL the time. I actually called her out on it.

Lastly, she was also actively "trying" to get the Lithuanian and me together, but she was trying a bit too hard. It was kind of her game. I knew she wanted me badly, and I wasn't going to fall for that. It was a pretty long set, altogether probably 45 minutes in the club.

At some point, since I had no wings around, I screened for a threesome:

"Have you girls ever kissed?"

They hadn't, and it turns out the Lithuanian had never kissed a girl and felt a little disgusted by the sheer thought of it. I see what's up and drop the topic. It's 3.30am, and it's about pulling time.

"I'm hungry, come with me."

I pull both, we walk out hand in hand. Logistics are a big part of the game, and they start now. I know the Lithuanian isn't down, and that the blonde one is, but I can't just ditch one. So I try to get them both into the cab - we were going to "go eat yogurt at a cool place, believe it or not, just 5min away."

Then a bit of bullshit starts. The Lithuanian freaks out when we're about to go into the cab, the blonde is kinda cool with it, but not happy because of her Lithuanian friend. She can't just go with me and ditch the friend. So I stop insisting on the cab and just start to walk with them in a random direction to chill them out.

The Lithuanian gives me some shit about the blonde not actually liking me, yet all that while she's talking, I'm holding hands with the blonde, haha. The Danish girl even says that's not true, that she does like me, but they can't just go to my place, etc... I'm a little lost, but then a great idea comes to me:

"Ok, look, here's the plan. We will all walk Greta (the Lithuanian girl) home and then I'll walk Frida (the Dane) home. Then I'll go find my bike and drive home myself. But first, food time!"

They agree.

In my mind, a funny pic of Borat appears: "Wawa-wiwa, great success!"

So we get some food and walk the Lithuanian girl home.

The blonde actually lives very close, no need for a cab, so we just head there. I try to make out two times on the way there, but she wouldn't. In retrospect, I didn't need to do that. She liked me enough and we were going towards her place, there was no need to try to make out in the cold and rain outside. There's always room for improvement in the game.

I remain chill and walk with her. She clearly mentioned she doesn't want to fuck that night. It's always a good sign when they say that. It means they're thinking about it. I also jokingly insist that "I'm on my period," and that "I am still a virgin, and so you should keep your hands off me."

We come to her door, I ask if I can pee. She invites me in and gives me some water. I ask her if she can show me her room, she does so, but a little hesitantly. We sit on the bed and just talk a little, nothing sexual. Then I gently touch her neck.

"Stop it." I stop.

I talk a bit again and then touch her neck again. I see she likes it, she's melting under my fingers. She tells me to stop again.

"But do you like it?"

"Yes."

I touch her face, very softly, very gently. She loves it. She tells me how she made a pact to herself - no more one night stands. "That's cool, we don't have to have sex if you don't want to. Come, let's just cuddle a bit."

I turn off the big light, turn on the small one, and lie next to her.

More touching, and then I proceed to feel her stomach and ass a bit. Oh my god, she really had a beautifully fit stomach and a very tight ass. And I loved how she was melting under my touch.

Then I ask her to remove her top (I had taken mine off beforehand) to be more comfortable. More passionate touching follows, and then I kiss her. It felt amazing, it was now about 5am, I was in bed with a beautiful girl and we were making out. Sometimes, it still blew my mind.

And then slowly but surely, our movements went from slow and gentle, to more rapid and forceful. All of our clothes came off, and I started to finger her pussy as she was giving me a blowjob. Her lips felt really good on my dick, and she was good at it too. I started to moan and get tense. She was soaking wet under my fingers too. There was a red, almost rose-like blush on her cheeks.

I take a condom and put it on.

There's no objections from her side. I bite her ear as I put my dick inside her. God, she was so wet, and it felt so good. Then I start to penetrate her faster and faster, and she starts being really loud. The bed is making really loud noises too.

"Do you want to fuck me from behind?"

And then she presents her perfect ass to me by positioning herself on her knees and elbows, so I could see her pink pussy perfectly. My hormones started raging. I slapped her ass as she was into that kind of stuff and then fucked her really hard until she came.

I give her a minute to breathe and then just as I am about to come myself something funny happens.

The bed breaks.

She laughs and tells me it's a funny bed and that it wasn't the first time. I get relieved, I thought we actually broke it, haha. I ask her to finish me with her mouth and she's cool with that. I lie there, on the half-broken bed, while this gorgeous blonde is sucking my dick.

I came quite fast because I was so excited, and she swallows all the cum too. What a feeling! And there's another funny thing happening. She needs to wake up at 6.30, which is in 45 minutes. So I lie there in the bed with her for a bit, kiss her, and leave around 6.

Chapter Twenty-Three
TOURISTS GET HIGH

Amsterdam, January 2016

I'm at the Amsterdam airport waiting for Max. My flight was a few hours earlier than his. Weirdly enough, I am sort of nervous. No, nervous isn't the right word. It was almost like there were butterflies in my stomach, kinda like when waiting for the date. Sounds super gay, but that's how it was.

It was partly me really looking forward to seeing him again, and partly me wanting to prove myself again, especially because my flights were paid for now. And a part of me also wondered in what state Max will be. Is he out of his gloomy and depressing mood, or is it still the same?

I see him, we fist bump and bro hug, and then we're off on the train to the city. The first hour or so I can feel a slight uneasiness, and he talks a lot. I already knew this about him. When around new people or when slightly uneasy, he'd talk more.

He talks about his experiences, how he chilled out a lot. Kind of expanded on our bits of C & C talk. A lot of eating, getting high, jerking off. He even went out once or twice. How he had some therapy calls, how he feels better now.

And he did look a lot better.

Then very soon, we're back to the old waters, just hustling and trolling around. We decided to use our first night in Amsterdam to get high together. We drop our bags in the Airbnb, and then walk towards the first coffee shop we can find. We (well, Max) buys a joint and start smoking and get really high, really fast.

Max opens two Israeli chicks sitting close to us and I join in. It goes nicely, but becomes super awkward at some point. Yeah, it was my bad.

You see, I was blocking the entrance with my chair, because I positioned myself closer to the girls after Max opened, so I could chat the other girl up. And for some reason, the dude working there got really pissed. Like he directly insisted I move my chair back to the other table, which would totally cut me off from the girls.

Add to this, that I was HIGH out of my mind and therefore not the most socially-capable person ever. So I try to reason with the guy who is getting more and more angry, and at some point, basically the whole coffee shop is staring at us. The girls are getting nervous, I am just pissed off at the guy, and Max is still talking to the girls. Or better said, at the girls, just like nothing happened. There's some mad iciness to that.

Anyway, obviously the set didn't go too well, after my battle of wits with the coffee shop dude.

Later, Max and I briefly discussed the interaction and I did agree that I kind of fucked it up there, and that Israeli girls were pretty down and we could both be banging them had I reacted differently. But then again, we also agreed that I was really high and that the guy was being a big dick too.

So we end up doing the second thing every tourist does in Amsterdam after they get high, search for the nearest shop to raid for junk food.

We buy everything.

Pizzas, chocolates, crisps, literally everything. And then we get lost in the shop and share quite a few laughs on the same account. Being lost in the shop, holding so many food bags that they are literally falling out of your hands, and laughing your ass off. Good times. I wonder what the shop owners must think when they see people like us, haha.

Back in the flat, we fire up our laptops for some serious Command & Conquer action, watch some funny movies and then eat even more. I think Max even did a Periscope session while we were still somewhat high, and he talked about how I liked girls with big boobs.

"So my Periscope friends, before I go, I'd like to ask you a question. Do you prefer boobs or ass in a girl?"

"You see, I've always been an ass guy, I really like skinny girls. But my assistant Bostjan, well, he's the typical boob guy."

"Whenever I see a chick that is slightly chubby, it's a red light for me, I will socialize with her, but I don't want to sleep with her. But for Bostjan, it's easy. He'd say something like:

"Yeah, I know man, but did you see her titties?"

"OMG! And he's good to go."

"I wish I would be like that sometimes..."

And the hearts start pouring out of Periscope, signaling that the audience likes Max when he talks about random funny shit too. I find it very amusing as well, despite kind of being an ass guy myself too.

It's not all about technique and game tactics, it's also about living the life and having some fun.

Max always surprises me when I think I can't be surprised anymore. In the middle of Amsterdam, high as hell, he'd still bust out a Periscope session, to build his brand, and even more so, to connect with his audience. That was really cool.

It was an awesome night all in all, full of laughing and bro bonding. I was really happy to be back on tour and I was really happy to be back around Max. But the best thing was, he really seemed to be feeling a lot better.

All that depressive mood and darkness, the positivity-sucking black hole, all that seemed to be gone.

At least for now.

Chapter Twenty-Four
HOW I HAD SEX WITH AN AMSTERDAM PROSTITUTE

Red Light District, Amsterdam, January 2016

I had this (not so secret) wish for quite some time. I guess this thought crosses the mind of most guys at some point. How it would be, to pay for sex? How it would be, to pick a stunning girl you like, pay her, and then have sex with her. No rejections, no smalltalk, straight to business.

It's a big taboo in most cultures. People don't talk about it, people don't write about it. It's shady. Yet it's all around us, it's in all of us, it is something primal that has been here all the time.

So I said to myself: *"Ok, dude, you're in Amsterdam, now's probably your best shot. If you don't do it now, you never will. It's legal here, you know the price, you know the spots, and it's safe as well: no need to worry about STDs or about getting robbed."*

And when you are at the point of doing it now or never, you should always go and do it. Otherwise, you might lose the chance and regret it for the rest of your life. So I had a couple of free hours on Saturday afternoon and I was like *"Fuck it, I'll do it."* I took a shower, put 70€ (Regular charge was 50€, but I might want something extra, haha) in my pocket, and got out on the street.

Our Airbnb is super central, so I walk for five minutes and start to see the red-lit windows. It's kinda like window shopping for clothes, but with girls inside. Some of them are on their phone, some of them are actively trying to make eye contact and invite guys in. Some of them are putting their makeup on, some of them just sit or stand, and look bored. Some of them are super hot, some of them not so much. They are from all ethnic and cultural backgrounds.

Now I'm starting to get more nervous. I'm checking the girls out. Not like in a club or on the street, where I am usually quite confident and take my time and feel comfortable checking out a girl I like. Here I'm afraid and shy. I don't really make eye contact and instead kinda check them out quickly before walking past. I make three circles around the busiest spots and in 15 minutes of walking I check out around 30 girls.

Slowly and steadily excuses are flowing into my mind. This always happens when you are about to do something, but are afraid. I go to the shop because I really had to buy some new lip balm. And then I visit a hotel to go to the toilet. I had to do it before, what if I needed to pee when getting busy with a girl? And then I mentally slap myself, I know I'm just procrastinating. The longer I wait, the harder it will be and the more stress I'll experience.

I know which girl I like and I head straight there.

I come to the window and take a last look at her before making a motion at her. She's got long, straight black hair. Not too tall, not too short. She's super skinny, a really fit body, nicely tanned, and with very sexy (later learned) fake tits. She also had super cool and sexy tattoos all over her right thigh, hip, and over her arms as well.

I also liked that she was just standing there – not checking her phone and also not trying too hard to get attention. She knew she was super hot and that guys will come. And when I looked her in the eyes she knew I wanted her, she smiled and opened the door.

I open the door and enter the small, dimly-lit room behind the window. It's warm and everything is glowing in neon red light. My heart is pounding, I haven't been this nervous in a long time.

"OK, baby, it's 50€ for a fuck and a blowjob, 15 minutes, OK?"

"OK."

I smile and close the door behind me.

I tell her that I'm nervous and that it's my first time.

"What's your name?"

We introduce ourselves and small talk for a minute or so,

that gets me a little more comfortable. I tell her I like her tattoos and that I just got my first one a couple of months ago in Bulgaria and show it to her.

"Really? I'm from Bulgaria..."

We talk about Sofia and Varna and how you get addicted to getting tattoos. I am a little less nervous, and a little more comfortable.

"All right, baby, just relax, take off your clothes, put them there, and then lie on the bed, OK?"

We both strip, and I lie on the bed. She quickly sprays disinfectant on my genitals, wipes it, and then puts a condom on my dick. She starts to give me a blowjob with the condom on, but my dick isn't really hard, I'm still very nervous.

A year or two ago that would suck. I would get angry at myself because I couldn't get it hard. And that doesn't really help with an erection problem and starts a vicious circle. Luckily, I now know better and just tell myself to relax, take my time, enjoy, and breathe deeper.

I tell her to position herself differently (while she's giving me head) so I could see her sexy ass and pussy, and touch her slim hips and boobs, which are super amazing. I tell her how much I love her boobs and ask her if they are real.

"No, they're fake. It's quite a good job, don't you agree?"

I agree and we both laugh. Then she continues the blowjob.

My dick is semi-hard now, and since the clock is ticking I

tell her to go on her knees. I grind myself against her ass, which is super erotic. Also, I notice how warm her body is to my touch. Then I penetrate her and for a few seconds it feels amazing. And then it's not amazing anymore, but just good. My dick is still not very hard. Oh well.

While having sex I notice her moaning is a bit robotic and forced. Some thoughts race through my head and I wonder if she ever enjoys her job. I am far from having the best sex of my life, yet it's still enjoyable. The thing that amazes me more is how aesthetically crazy I am about her beautiful body.

Also, there are all kinds of things I want to do to her, that I normally do when having sex, but those things are off limits now. I want to kiss her, I want to touch her pussy, I want to hold her body close and tight to me, I want to kiss and bite her neck, shoulders, and back. I want to slap her ass. I want to feel the warmth of her body and look into her eyes when I fuck her.

"Baby, you'll have to come for me soon..."

Yeah, the clock was ticking, lol. So I started to jerk myself off and then asked her to help me finish just before I came. It felt good, like all orgasms do. She then took some paper towels and removed the condom. We both put our clothes on. She kisses me on the cheek and says goodbye.

When I step outside, I feel beyond amazing, a wide smile on my face. It was 20% due to just having an orgasm, 20% due to being in a company of a super hot girl (although slightly diminished because it was paid for) and 60% because of overcoming fear, and realizing a desire you have had for a long time.

I'm super glad I went. But I doubt I'll visit again anytime soon. I just prefer a girl who likes me too. I like sharing the amazing intimacy and connection, kissing, biting and all the rest that comes together with amazing sexual partners.

And I don't think I can do without cuddling either.

Chapter Twenty-Five
JOHAN BLOWS MY MIND

Amsterdam, January 2016

One of the main reasons that I loved my job was because I got to meet awesome people. And in Amsterdam, on the last day there, I met Max's German marketer, Johan.

Max was just about to create and launch his first online product, called *"The Natural."* The Natural would later on become the best-selling RSD product, something that would turns the live of many guys around. A player's encyclopedia, if you will. And Max wanted his own marketer too, he didn't want just the guy RSD had at that moment. And well, that conversation seriously blew my mind.

I was always interested in learning how to sell, how to market, how to make a story appealing. How to show the best sides, how to use catchy phrases, how to awaken the deep and secret wishes of the potential client, all of that and more. And the conversation in Amsterdam was an information overload, a bomb of amazing and lucrative cheat codes.

"So look Max, for the average YouTube user, the retention rate is 35%. That means they watch, on average, 35% of the videos. So what you have to do is look at your videos which have 50%+ retention rate and see what works in them. And then you want to maximize the YouTube search engine optimization for those videos, because they will bring in the most leads.

Regarding the YouTube Search Engine Optimization, I want you to shoot the Manifesto, your longest and most in-depth video, as soon as possible, way before we start the launch period. Because that will get a ton of views on YouTube and again, bring a lot of fresh viewers to the sales funnel.

Also, we'll make sure we use a lot of colloquial words in the title of the manifesto in some other speculated high viewership videos, so they bring in fresh people, the ones who don't know about RSD yet, from YouTube's organic search..."

Right now I can't really recall everything that I learned or heard there. But there was a swirl of phrases such as sales funnel, the plan of trailers and videos, basic pricing plans, pitching strategy, decision trees, unique selling points, cross collaborations, and more.

They talked about how the content might and probably will be leaked, and how to prevent it, the strengths and weakness of other RSD products, the style of releasing Max's product. All while being super honest and brutally real.

They mentioned a lot of other people in the game, some other non-RSD coaches who run their own companies.

Johan had worked with a lot of them before. He explained the difference between their lifestyles and their selling points, and how Max can use that knowledge to maximize the spreading of his product.

They talk about search engine optimization and social media, how to use Periscope effectively, and how to get the cross promotion videos going on. They talk about various analytic tools, how to measure engagement, and what to do with the data.

Two or three hours passed just like that. I was making notes all the time. Meanwhile, I was screaming in my mind:

"Oh Shit. OHHH SHIT! This is so fucking cool, omg, my life is fucking amazing. This is the golden nugget right there, these guys really know how to fucking make money, omg, my assistantship was the best decision of my life, fuck, I'm gonna cum in my pants..."

That was some really cool information right there, and I had a feeling that a time would soon come when I would be in need of marketing knowledge myself.

But until then, let me just enjoy the ride.

Chapter Twenty-Six
MAX'S DAY GAME PULL

Vienna January 2016

After Amsterdam, Max and I went to Vienna.

It was a lot more chill this time. No Hot Seats, no Free Tours, just the Bootcamp. So during the week we just hit the gym a lot and did some work. I finally had enough time to meditate, and even do a bit more of my remote-based work.

We played some C & C, and I went pimping with one of Max's ex-wings that visited us during a computer game session. It was pretty good, and we actually took 2 girls on an instant date.

Instant Date
Usually happens when day gaming. After screening the girls and seeing that they have some time on their hands, you can instantly take them to a coffee shop, to the park, or

wherever you want to go. Since you just met them a few minutes ago, this is called an instant date.

However, I was noticing something was a bit off with me.

I still gamed, but I didn't chase every girl I saw like before. It was as if there was a hidden force slowing me down. It had been about 2 weeks since I got laid, if we don't count the prostitute experience in Amsterdam. Usually, I'd get jittery and start to pimp it hard. But this time, I didn't mind so much. And occasional texting and back-and-forth picture sending with Alex helped too...

Sunday's Bootcamp was pretty epic. Max was teaching day game. He was still rocking it hard, but had a little less edge than usual. At some point while filming, I see a super hot brunette, and I point her out to him:

"Hey Max, what about that one?"

"Damn, she's hot. Yeah, let's do it."

He walks in her direction, speeds up a little bit so he is in front of her, and then casually opens her, saying something in German. She seems a little bit startled, but still politely answers. I can hear everything in my headphones, since Max's mic transmits the sound to the camera I hold. I don't understand everything, but I feel like she's not super open.

But Max just keeps it cool and continues to playfully chat in an easy-going vibe. In a minute or two, the girl opens up and starts to be really responsive to his gentle teasing. For example, when he teases her about her fur coat, and how they had to kill a lot of cute bunny rabbits to create it, she pokes his shoulder, etc.

They proceed to talk about where's she's from (she's Portuguese) and how she ended up in Vienna. Max tells her a bit about himself, and how Vienna is a place where he used to live as a student, and a bit about his world travels. He also screens logistics and figures out she has some time on her hands.

On one hand, the whole thing didn't surprise me anymore, and on the other, I was still blown away. This short, bearded, Austrian guy, just chatting up an absolute bomb on the street, and have her giggle and open up to him in less than ten minutes. Crazy!

Also, I had one of the Bootcamp students with me, so I shared one of the headphones with him, so he could listen in too, and get some of the verbal game Max was doing. There was also Max's old wing accompanying us. After 10 or 15 minutes of walking and chatting, Max suggests grabbing some coffee. The girl happily agrees, and they bounce to Starbucks.

Such a sigh, haha. Max bringing his girl to instant date in Starbucks, and 3 guys with a camera following them, as if nothing was happening. You can imagine I was super good and very discrete by this point, so nobody actually figured I have a video camera on me.

Here's the catch. It looked like a photo camera, there were no lights flashing, and I held it in a super matter-of-fact way, like it's just hanging there, like I wasn't even paying attention to it. It seems I was doing well, since no one almost ever noticed. It was still scary sometimes, especially in day game, but I was becoming quite a pro at it.

We're in the Starbucks for 40 minutes or so, we're sipping our own coffee which feels nice, Vienna was cold in

January. I adjust the camera settings from time to time, but it's pretty chill most of the time. I like steady shots. Then I hear that Max is planning to bounce her, probably going for the pull. I signal the guys to get ready. Max and the girl leave, we wait for a minute or so, to not be too obvious, and then leave as well.

I receive an angry WhatsApp from Max:

"Where the fuck are you, man, I'm about to pull and you're not here, what the fuck, come quick!"

"Behind you, bro, we're already outside, just went out the other way. Ready to go. Also, fix your mic wire, because the sound is breaking a bit."

So Max leads the girl towards our Airbnb (this time I got the couch since Vini was not around yet), and the 3 guys follow. This is fucking epic. I am recording a sick day game pull of an absolute hottie, from open all the way to the house. None of the other coaches have that, that is simply epic. I'm super careful, and super nervous, because the sound is somewhat messing with us.

I hear Max seeding the pull:

"Yeah, you haven't seen Matrix? That's crazy. I totally have to show the opening scene with the red and blue pill to you, it's awesome. But hey, only if you promise you're nice, I can't just take any girl to my place."

Okay, this will be the moment of truth, I have to get ready to get the pull shot, which means filming how she enters the flat with him. We never film beyond that point, since it's not a public space anymore and would interfere with privacy issues.

And by the way, just so you know, we always hide the identity of the girls by blurring their faces, so nobody can recognize them. The main point of having videos like that, is that guys can see exactly what Max does, and try to replicate it. Another reason is that a video like that blows their reality. For most non-players, it's virtually impossible to believe that a regular guy could meet a girl during the day, and bring her to his place in a matter of hours.

Well, a video like that says "fuck you" to reality and to all the chodes, and shows what is actually possible if you have tight game.

So yeah, Max walks through the door, the girl follows, and I record, and even close up with perfect focus, and in a few seconds the sound breaks as the distance increases.

I just successfully recorded one of Max's full day game pulls. More than an hour long, this was the first complete day game pull, from the open, to instant date, to a private location. No other coach has that.

Not bad.

Chapter Twenty-Seven
HEARTACHE

Copenhagen, January 2016

Copenhagen was the last city Max and I hit before Vini joined us. I was missing the bearded Brazilian, and was looking forward to seeing him the week after.

I felt weirdly at home in Copenhagen. We switched so many cities and countries in so little time, that I got adjusted to places really fast. All it took was a few familiar streets and clubs and I felt almost at home, or at least not totally alienated.

Copenhagen, similar to Amsterdam and Vienna, had only Bootcamps. As in Vienna, we hit the gym regularly, ate clean, and handled the whole work/life balance pretty well. We actually had time to catch up with some friends, mainly a cool photographer who helped Max promote his Instagram profile. We even did a 3-way C & C battle, that was really fun!

But gradually, the funny feeling about game from Vienna returned and became stronger.

I didn't even feel like gaming that much. I didn't feel like running after girls every second of my free time, or even during grocery runs, etc. And I wondered what had changed.

From time to time, I wanted to go meet and talk to a girl, but then decided not to, because it felt like too much effort. From time to time, Alex would come to my mind.

It was just so much nicer with her. She knew me, I knew her. I knew how to turn her on, she knew how to make me want her. I knew we were gonna have an awesome time together, and that she wouldn't give me any shit.

Most of all, I knew I would see her again.

You see, if I wanted to meet a new girl, a lot of things needed to happen. First I'd have to open her, be cool, and talk to her. And then I'd have deal with all the logistics, make her comfortable, share my story, make sure all is good, listen to her story, etc.

And only then would we maybe be able to have a kick ass time hanging out, which only maybe would result in intimacy and sex. And then, even if all went well, and we'd enjoy each other, I would probably never see that girl again.

And that sucked hardcore.

It was kind of like offering your soul on a silver platter, and then waiting for it to get crushed, over and over and over again. Finally, I understood why sometimes Max didn't want to go out and pimp it, when he had a night off. How he didn't want to go on that Tinder date, even if the sex was almost guaranteed.

I finally understood what girls meant when they said: *"I'm not looking to meet anyone right now."*

I was somehow less horny. I mean, I'm not saying I was a monk, I still opened a hot chick or two every now and then, I still had a date in each city, but it was way different. *Waaaay different.*

At the time, I also started to focus on my videos a lot more, on my work for the other company, and my own emerging blog and YouTube channel – BossLifeHacks. I paid more attention to getting good nutrition and hitting the gym. I was meditating more or less regularly around that time too!

And it felt fucking good. It felt centered and like a part of me was recovering.

I was, in a way, starting to notice a big wound inside of me. A wound that had emerged from opening myself up completely in new romantic relationships beyond count. A wound that deepened every time I would leave, and throw the last relationship away. You could say I was hitting an "emotional gym" on steroids for the past half a year.

And that taught me a lot.

In a short amount of time, I gained a world of experience, and a world of pain.

I knew what I was looking for in a girl. I knew the time and effort it would take to seduce her. I knew my emotional input if I decided to go for it.

And based on my current condition, which was physically rested but emotionally wounded, I decided to pass up the opportunity most of the time.

Chapter Twenty-Eight
FRIENDS REUNITED AND A PROMISE TO BE HELD

New York, February 2016

In New York City, we met Vini again.

I remember seeing him there, at the JFK airport. He looked the same, but more rested, and with a shorter beard. And his Jedi braid was missing too. I gave my Brazilian bro a big bear hug, and then proceeded to troll with him and Max as we usually did.

That was a happy day, and we reconnected fast.

However, NYC was really busy. We had the full deal: Bootcamp, Free Tour, and the Hot Seat. Not to mention that getting from point A to point B in NYC is not the easiest thing in the world. There was a lot of work to do: grocery runs, getting things ready for the events, filming, editing, and more. I wanted to shoot a very cool personal video in Times Square too.

So there I was, back on the road, with a shitload of work and extra things I wanted to do, and the typical thing happened.

I got sick.

I have to praise my pharmaceutical geekiness and the mighty supplement called N-Acetyl Cysteine, an amino acid supplement which boosts the body's natural antioxidant production. Even Max and Vini started to take it after some time. That totally saved my ass, but even with that, I was walking around half-drugged and in zombie mode.

Yet, the energy of NYC overcame the tiredness. The city is just freaking awesome. It's big, it's alive, it's… it's New York! So even though I could feel the burnout coming back, even though I could see it coming back in Max and Vini too, I still felt so grateful to find myself in NYC, on the other side of the world.

And all this happened, because I decided to join a dating coach on his adventures. Sometimes I just sit and wonder at the beauty and complexity of life. It's so majestic that thinking about it for too long makes my eyes water.

There were a lot of cool things that happened in NYC.

It was Alex's birthday in the middle of the week, so I did something really cool. I went to the top of my host's rooftop apartment in Manhattan, overseeing the Chrysler building, took out a selfie stick and sang the happy birthday song. In the middle of the song I kind of stripped, so I was topless, I thought it was kind of sexy and kind of funny. It was mainly cold though, as it was a windy winter's day in NYC.

However, the video struck home, as it got a lot of likes and comments when posted on her FB timeline. Moreover, Alex really liked it, and then sent me a sweet voice message full of happy thoughts, and finished off with some sentences and pictures that made my dick really hard.

Next off, Vini and I had the best midnight munchies at his host's workplace. We finished recording my personal vid in Times Square late at night on Sunday. Vini's host was with us, and then for some reason, even though he was socially slightly awkward, he invited us to his workplace for a free meal. Keep in mind it was 2am.

So we roll up into this start-up tech company that was open all the time and offered free food to their employees (and apparently to their employees' friends too). That was the best meal I had in some time. Unlimited food, and since it was a new-age, hippy startup, there was plenty of healthy food too. Carrot sticks and hummus, low-carb granola and protein bars, cheese and oven baked crisps, yogurt and more goodies. That was a feast.

Possibly the favorite experience was when Vini and I had a beer after the Hot Seat on Saturday. Again, we were cleaning up and shooting the testimonials till about 1am, so Max told us we didn't have to come and shoot the rest of the Bootcamp that night. Since the event was at very fancy hotel with an even fancier rooftop that included a 360-degree rotating restaurant, we decided to have a drink up there.

Of course, being broke and unpaid (luckily travel expenses were paid now), we go for the cheapest $7 drinks, a beer for Vini and a homemade ice-tea for me. We even shoot a kick ass time-lapse of NYC from the rotating rooftop. And we have a conversation I will never forget:

"You know, bro, I like this city, it's crazy. I wonder where we will all end up after these travels. You know, after 3 weeks, I'll go to Brazil, and you back to London or Slovenia. I have no idea what's gonna happen. But I know I'll never be the same.

I wanna hustle now, bro, I want to have my own company, or at least work in a way I am self-sufficient and on my own terms. I don't wanna be broke anymore, I want to be able to afford a nice drink and food wherever in the world I am."

He hit dead centre with this. I got goose bumps and something deep inside me resonated with that thought completely. I was at a loss for words, so I just nodded and gave him a look that unmistakably meant I agree 100%. And then he continued with a great idea:

"You know bro, we'll probably never meet again. And I don't like that fact. I want to revive our old memories, man, how we traveled around, how we laughed at Max when he had his little tantrums, how we pulled those two Polish girls in Krakow. I wanna reminisce on all that.

Let's meet up again man, somewhere in the world."

It was a great idea, so I take a second to think and then reply:

"How about we meet up right here bro, in NYC, it is a pretty fucking epic place. And since we were both too broke to go up the Empire State building, let's have a drink up there. And stay at

some hotel close by, so we can pull there easily when we go pimping."

"I'm down. When do you think is a good time?"

"2020 bro, 2020 should be plenty of time for us to reach those goals."

And so it was agreed. We'd meet again, on top of the Empire State building, drinking a fancy drink, staying in an expensive hotel close by. Because why not, and because I knew we will both hustle hard enough to make it happen in the next few years...

Most of the time in NYC, I was super excited. The big city life was in me. I took pictures, made videos, chatted to all my friends about it. I ate the NYC "dogs" and the pizza. I saw the subway, I noticed that hip-hop culture truly lives in NYC.

For example, I heard a random dude on train talk about DJ Premier, one of my favorite DJs ever. And he talked about him as if he knew him, as if they grew up in the same block. NYC was more than awesome.

Yet, in addition to all of that, I was feeling a bit tired. I started to hate packing all of my stuff up so regularly. All I had was that fucking blue suitcase, and even the suitcase started to show signs of wear and tear. It was battered, missing a few clips, and had a few deep cuts running across it. I guess it was a metaphor for how I was.

I was starting to think about the end of the tour, and what would happen then. I was tired emotionally even more than physically, I just wanted less work, and more sleep. I didn't really pick up any girl in New York, although some of them hooked to my smile and all that.

Didn't even have a date.

And I could see the tiredness in Max and Vini too. It was a bit better after our rest. But it's like running. After a long run, you take a break and you feel good. But if you start running very soon again, the tiredness comes back quickly.

Chapter Twenty-Nine
ON BEING A RSD INSTRUCTOR

Miami, February 2016

Party in the city where the heat is on.
All night on the beach till the break of dawn.
Welcome to Miami (Bienvenido a Miami).
(Will Smith - Miami)

Miami was awesome, and probably my favorite city after Krakow. If I said that NYC was busy, it was still nothing compared to Miami - we had the RSD World Winter Summit there. Meaning Max had a five-day Bootcamp, he had a big speech to give, and on top of all that we had to do a bunch of cross-collaboration vids. First with every other RSD instructor and then some other guys from the self-development industry like Elliott Hulse, Big Brandon

Carter, and Kinobody.

I was lucky to be hosted by Ward, my friend from London who I did the "Bootcamp" for, at a super awesome location just 10 minutes' walk from the beach. So despite being really busy, I took my time and every day, after I woke up, went straight to the beach to catch some sun and a quick swim.

My joy and happiness were overwhelming. After a long and cold winter, walking around in just shorts and a tank top was like a miracle. The water was pleasantly warm and the ocean filled me with energy. There's a certain force to natural elements, the ocean being one of the most powerful for me. It's just so infinite, and freeing.

I remember a video I posted on my social media, I think I was really into catchy titles at the time so I named it *"Half-Naked Crazy Slovenian Dancing in Miami Beach, Florida."* My Facebook friends went crazy and I got thousands of views. So yeah, nothing to really complain about in Miami.

However, despite the happenings, a sort of haze was over me. I couldn't exactly say what it was, probably a mix of life on the tour, my heartache, plus some other undefinable factors. But the excitement of the big city life kind of helped holding that in check.

And it's good, because despite tiredness, there were numerous chances to prove myself in Miami. For example, I co-ran an actual Bootcamp with RSD Madison for a few hours.

Max was busy having a business dinner with potential YouTube cross-collaboration partners, and he asked me to meet the guys at the venue and start coaching them. He had never done that before, but he wanted to experiment a little. He would let his assistant do the prep job for him, so he could get more done for the brand in the long run.

So I met the guys and went to do the regular things. By now I know the prep work for each night really well. We talked about the night before, each student's sticking points, and things they need to improve on that night. The main thing is really just to just focus on the guy, listen, and then try to work on his issue specifically.

Then we go into different sets, I push them a little, and they mostly rock. I blew one of the guy's mind with a silent open. That was seriously funny, and cool. I had told him to open a girl without words and he wouldn't do it. Or more specifically, he had asked me to show him how. And that's fair enough. When you push someone to do something scary, you should ALWAYS be able to demonstrate the same thing.

Now, with game, you can't just go and get any girl, that's retarded. If she doesn't like you, she just doesn't like you, and there's no way you're getting with her. Which is totally cool. But it doesn't mean you can't go up to her and say "Hi" and see what the deal is.

So I go to open this girl, I'll do a fully silent open, no words. Just laser eye contact and hand gestures. I approach the set, go straight to the girl, smile, and motion her to take my hand. She does and I gently drag her into a hug, she hugs me back.

I smile and motion a "Hello" to her friends. And then, very elegantly and slowly, I take her hand, maintain strong eye contact and a smile, and lead her away from her friends towards the sofas where we lie down together in an embrace.

Now I kinda fucked it up later, I pushed for the make out too early, but the guy's mind was already blown anyway. And at that point I realized that I had done something pretty cool.

Just a regular dude, a young guy from Slovenia, dressed in an H & M shirt and pants, and Primark (cheap) shoes. Walking up to a super hot girl in a posh club in Miami Beach, taking her hand without words, leading her away from her friends, and lying down in an embrace together. Dude, if that was caught on a camera, it would be some pretty epic footage.

And that got me thinking about the RSD Instructor position. It wasn't the first time that I had this thought, it had popped out a few times during the whole tour. But in Miami, it was pretty strong. Why? Because I saw The Lifestyle.

I saw how RSD as an organization runs, and I saw the rockstar status the instructors have there. A lot of people pay them very good money in addition to kissing their asses. And really successful people, some of who just happen to suck with girls, they want to get in on the party too. So not only do you get paid for teaching game, which is awesome beyond your wildest dreams, you also get to network with some of the most successful people in the world.

My mind was racing on several occasions in Miami, because you see, there was a crushing dilemma in my mind.

I knew I had what it takes. I had seen how Max works, I

knew the process. I was already shooting one video in each city that we visited, despite having a shitload of other work. I knew how to run a Bootcamp, I am good at public speaking. I was an insider, I'd just have to make an offer RSD couldn't refuse, and I would be in.

However, I knew the dark side as well.

There's a lot of work. Insane amounts to be honest, way more than any 9-5. It would basically be a year or two of suffering. Every week the country would change, and a new Hot Seat, Bootcamp, and Free Tour would have to be run. First, though, I'd have to record a lot of infield footage and create compilations, etc. Rinse and repeat for months, even a year or two, who knows.

And then, as if that's not bad enough, RSD would take a big cut of the earnings - after I'd finally start to get any earnings, that is. The first six months or so you work for free. I mean, obviously that's how companies work. They give you a big ass YouTube list in exchange for a part of the revenue you create, but still.

And all of that, I could probably handle. But there were even darker facts.

You put your face on YouTube. And it's not just regular YouTube. You see, the way this works is, you need to have infield footage. Clips of you making out with girls, clips of you pulling the girls. Otherwise nobody would believe you. It's the cost of entry in this field.

And that makes it a real problem when you meet a girl you really like. Try to love a girl and explain to her how much you love her, while she sees you pulling other girls on YouTube. She can rewind and replay it over and over...

Even with Alex, for example. I really liked her, and she liked me. And she knew I get with some other girls sometimes, and she was cool with that. But I'd never rub it in her face, that would be a super dick move. However, if I had infield clips on YouTube, she could play it over and over again. She'd actually get to see other girls that I had sex with.

And that's tough to swallow. Even for the most open-minded girls.

In addition, I had heard so many "dark stories" of RSD instructors' lives that it was crazy. No wonder people get fat, negative, and depressed on the tour. It's fucking rough.

Why don't you try to eat clean and workout regularly during the weekly flights, Bootcamps, Free Tours, and Hot Seats, AND the content creation. And don't forget you probably will want to lay a few girls too, but just to spice it up, you won't really get to see them again for months, if at all.

So there were these two conflicting thoughts I was having. One side of me wanted to become an instructor really badly, and the other was trying to keep me away from it.

Maybe mostly because in my head, to this day, I actually believe I have what it takes. But finally I realized and decided that the perceived downsides were too great. I didn't want to kill myself touring for a year or two. I didn't want to have the emotional drama and trauma just to prove something to myself. I didn't want this controversy in my life.

So after much thought I was done with the dilemma. It

was one of the hardest decisions in my life. I battled my ego and parts of me that really wanted all of that. A sort of calmer, and maybe an older part of me took the command and helped me enforce the decision. It was still painful on a few more occasions, and I silently wondered what would have happened if I had gone for it. But I never really thought about actually doing it ever again.

Anyway.

Max, Vini, and I were in a pretty good state. However, writing this sentence down speaks of the actual state of things. We were on the edge, fueled by Miami and having a lot of things to do, and Max's burning vision and ambition.

It's crazy, how one man's ideas and vision can propel whole groups of people and even organizations to spend every bit of energy they have and commit to following and making that same dream happen. Max is definitely one of the greatest leaders I know.

And in case you were wondering, yes, girls in Miami are really damn hot. But I didn't get laid. The feelings of heartache from Copenhagen and Vienna persisted. I went out a night or two, either after the Bootcamp or on a night off, but didn't pull. Don't get me wrong, I wanted to. But it seemed I just didn't have it in me at the time, the killer instinct was gone.

I met a super awesome and hot French-Canadian girl at the beach with my flatmate, I took her contact info and put her into my "How to get a Dream Job" video, but that's about it regarding the girls in Miami for me. No banging, not even a kiss.

No wait, that's not true.

I actually pulled off a pretty cool threesome make out on the last night of the Bootcamp. Vini was filming that night, it was a Sunday and we were in some super hot beach club. I saw two hotties dancing on a table. I wave to one, get her to help me get up with them. Dance with them, then make out with both.

Dudes around me, most of them RSD fans, couldn't believe their eyes. I got an ego spike, but then I had to go back to the Bootcamp.

And well, that was that regarding girls and me for Miami.

Chapter Thirty
AUSTIN PLANS &
KOMBUCHA

Austin, March 2016

The next was Austin, Texas, a really chilled out place.

No events, just the Bootcamp. We were all pretty tired and were looking forward to the end of the tour. A lot of the times you could hear us saying things like; *"Once the tour is over…"* or *"I can't wait to live somewhere again…"* We were casting out our thoughts into the future.

And we spent so much time together, that we knew each other's thoughts quite well, so here's what was going on in our heads.

Max had the clearest path. After the tour, he was focusing all his forces on recording *The Natural*, his first product that would *"end the pickup world as we know it."* Pretty catchy slogan, no? The plan for him was to move to Austria and stop teaching, focusing for three months solely on the product, and then start a short release/promotion tour.

Vini was going back to Brazil. It was his Visa situation, plus he had been working for Max for over a year now. He needed some time off. He wanted to focus on himself and his life. And I could really understand how he felt. I knew that he also had some RSD instructor aspirations in the past, I think every assistant does. Plus, Vini was a killer in the game. However, his aspirations changed too.

As for me, I didn't have a clue what to do. I was kinda open to working on *The Natural* with Max. I knew that Vini would have priority to join the small in-house crew, but I didn't think he was down to do that. He'd had enough of RSD for some time.

I remember I struggled with the decision at the time. I knew Max would need someone to help with *The Natural*, and I knew it would be paid this time. I wasn't sure if I wanted to do it though. I had a lot of aspirations on starting solo, or focusing on the other remote job too. You see, the whole world tour awoke a burning ambition inside of me. I wanted to get rich and successful, fast.

I roughly knew what was on the table. Three months of hard, yet interesting work, some good money, yet living in a remote alpine village in Austria. I had a few Skype calls with some of my friends and business buddies to determine the best course of action and then made my decision.

I had a talk with Max, there in our Airbnb in Austin, and we agreed that I would help him out with the product: shooting, editing, doing everything I could assist with. We also agreed on some points like having a decent paycheck and some off-time, so we didn't burn ourselves out again.

Other than that, nothing particularly crazy happened in Austin. I mean, if you take in the fact that running after an elite dating coach with a camera inside of the world's most prestigious nightclubs is no biggie.

Well, I did have the best BBQ ribs of my life in Austin, and I was amazed by the "no guns" signs in front of public spaces. You see, you don't get that in Europe. Nobody except the army, police, an odd hunter or two (and criminals) carry guns in Europe.

I remember going exercising with Vini and drinking a lot of Kombucha. Max had a thing for Kombucha, and he'd have me buy whole cases of it, for all of us. He told us a story of how he really liked it, and how he was too broke to buy it when he was assisting himself. And he had made a pact to himself, that he would become successful enough so he could have Kombucha in unlimited amounts. You see, it's the small things that matter. And now, whenever I see Kombucha, I remember Austin.

Regarding girls in Austin, I only had one date with a really cute girl there, but we didn't even make out.

So you see, we were tired and we had heavy thoughts about the future; it would be quite uneasy for all of us. Adding the knowledge that we would soon be splitting after six months or so of being together practically every day, wasn't helping.

I had a feeling it would get slightly emotional.

Chapter Thirty-One
THE BOSTON WEED PARTY

Boston, March 2016

Boston was the last city of our tour, and after that Max and I would fly to Austria to work on *The Natural*, and Vini would fly back to Brazil.

There was nothing special about Boston, I didn't like it that much. Maybe because I was so tired. The girls weren't hot, and you couldn't go out anywhere on a Thursday night - I tried. And everything else kind of disappeared from my memory.

Everything except the goodbye.

The night before the final one in Boston, after Bootcamp, Max invites Vini and I to a sort of goodbye dinner. It was a cool place, some gourmet pizzeria in Boston. Max's host joined us too. We had an epic time: the food was amazing, we chilled and trolled, and even had some shots after.

Vini and I wanted to get drunk together for once, because we hadn't managed to do that... well, ever. This tells you about the amount of hustling we had been doing in our jobs, haha.

In the end we didn't get that drunk, but we did smoke some weed and had an epic time. We laughed a lot and started to wander around the city, which was super dead. I know it was Sunday night, but still, Boston is a big city.

A perfect moment I will remember forever was when Max's host brought out a shiny, gold $1 coin. Us being high, we were just staring at the coin in amazement for a few moments.

"Dudeeeee, check it out, it's fucking gold. Wooooow."

I didn't even know they existed. And then Vini, being a funny Brazilian, tried to persuade Max's host to trade the coin for a $1 bill. Max and I laughed so hard we almost cried when we saw how serious he was with that.

Later on I learned that the whole dinner had cost Max like $200. Max covered it all and I was once again surprised. Vini and I worked really hard for Max. But in return, we learned and experienced a lot. And more importantly, Max really cared about us. And it felt good to know that.

The last night we already had all of our shit packed, so we had some time to kill. Max always had a thing for cinemas, and would invite Vini and I to a movie several times during the tour. So we went to the cinema together for the last time. The movie we watched was *"10 Cloverfield Lane."* a sort of scary psychological thriller that actually sort of matched the mood.

We trolled before the movie, like we always did, a lot of bullshit here and there but the feeling of departure was hovering over all of us. We knew we would part ways after this evening, and that it was gonna be weird and difficult.

The movie was pretty dark. A story about two people being caught in a basement with a psychotic guy, who thought the outside world was dominated by aliens. A lot of blood, violence, and silent scenes.

When it ended, we went out and it was time for goodbyes. Max and I shared the Airbnb, because it was booked under my name this time. So Vini would go back to his host after, and then fly back to Brazil the next morning, whereas Max and I would fly to Austria together.

"Get Dooooown, Enough Talk..." *"Into the chopper, aaaaa..."*

Funny Arnold Schwarzenegger quotes would signal the start of our trolling like always. Add some Borat in, some funny Chinese impersonations, and the GLA Terrorists voices from C & C and you have a proper troll party.
However, our voices were not quite as happy or as funny as usual. We knew that someone would have to stop the joking and say some real words, and then goodbye would come. I was thinking about breaking the trolling mood and telling Vini I'd miss him, and that we should stay in touch.

But I learned a thing or two about goodbyes, even before starting to work with Max. When lives go different ways, there's no staying in touch. You may want to, but it just doesn't work that way. You stay in touch if you have regular things to do together - work, dance, play a game, etc. Any ritual or habit that brings you together. Otherwise, the relationship usually doesn't last, be it friends or intimacy based.

I mean, if there's a very strong bond such as in family or years of friendship, that's different. But even these massively strong friendship bonds sometimes don't last so well. Time just changes a lot of things.

The three of us had all been through so much together, it was incredible.

We pimped at crazy prestigious night club parties together. We pulled together, we laughed together, and we cried together. We worked hard together, we were sick together, we worked almost till the point of passing out together. We knew basically everything about each other, we knew when one of us REALLY liked a girl, we knew when someone was in a bad mood or pissed off.

We were really bonded.

But I knew, deep in my heart, that after we stopped working together, we would split. We were just going in different directions. And there was nobody to blame for that. It's just how it is. There was also no need to feel sorry. We gave it our all when the time was right, and when it ends, it ends.

You see, all this was racing through my mind, and I'm guessing the guys had their own versions of something similar. And just as I was about to start saying goodbye, Max broke the silence and turned to Vini.

"Alright man, have safe travels, bro. We'll stay in touch regarding the videos anyway, right..."

I also said goodbye to Vini.

"Take care, man, I'll miss your hairy Brazilian ass. And besides, we'll stay in touch via WhatsApp anyway. And don't forget the New York City promise in about five years."

"I won't."

Then the Uber arrived. Max jumped in, I followed, and took one last look at Vini. As Max was giving directions to the driver, Vini walked away, and I haven't seen him since.

Chapter Thirty-Two
LESSONS LEARNED

Austria, April 2016

Flash forward a few weeks. I'm in Austria, in Max's flat. I just woke up, in my own room, and had a nice cup of coffee. I'm working on this book. After that, I'll have a lot of video editing to do for *The Natural*. Somewhere in between I'll go to the gym and then eat a healthy meal.

Once the main hustle of the day is done, towards the early evening, Max and I might play a game of Command & Conquer, or I'll work on my other business a little. Then I'd just chill, maybe cook some food, maybe read a bit, or watch a movie. Very relaxing, and in balance.

I am fantasizing about next week, when Alex is coming to visit for a few days. I talked to Max and we'll try to minimize my workload for a few days, plus he'll hook me up with one of his dad's apartments for the time. So good!

And then in the middle of these thoughts, the goosebumps hit me hard as I realize... I am happy.

I'm happy, healthy, calm, and peaceful.

A lot of the things can only be learned in retrospect, and a lot of the things that I learned on this crazy six-month traveling adventure, are only just starting to hit me...

Barcelona, July 2016

Flash forward again a few months, and I'm sitting in my flat in Barcelona, Spain.

I moved here for the summer, potentially longer. I am eating clean, I found some local breakdancers. I am learning Spanish and am working on my video skills, which is how I make a living now. I have my own room in the city centre, cool flatmates, and all the time in the world. You could say I have all the things I need to be happy. Again, you only learn things in retrospect.

Before coming here, and after finishing *The Natural* with Max, I was in London for two weeks. I guess a traveler's life will be hard to avoid after the World Tour. It's just so easy to book a ticket, board a plane, and emerge thousands of miles away in some different country...

I met Alex in London at the time too. We hung out quite a lot, and that was after she visited me in Austria for a few days in April. And I remember at some point she looks me in the eyes and tells me:

"You're somehow different from when I first met you. It's like you've changed. Like you've changed from a boy into a man."

The sentence might not seem like much, and she might not think of it as much then, but it rang long and hard inside of me. Because it struck something real.

I had grown a lot in those six months. And to be honest, not all the growth had been pleasant. I had learned a lot about myself and life in general.

My game is a lot more mature now.

I'm not a dancing monkey for the girls anymore. I feel a lot less fear. I know what to do. I just walk up to the girl, quite confidently, and start to chat, and then take it from there. I have a better intuition, and I understand the social circumstances more.

Most importantly, I don't stress about it. If it goes well, cool. If it doesn't, cool. Furthermore, I even see girls differently now. I focus much more on the girls I really want to meet, instead of the quantity.

I know exactly what I want in a girl now: a hot, sporty body, she needs to like healthy food and exercise, and she needs to be very open in bed. I also want the girl to be very feminine, to take care of me, and to be the feminine pole to my masculine drive.

I learned how to hustle too, this, maybe was the biggest thing I took away.

I can now easily work focused for six, up to ten, hours in a day. Before the tour I would start cracking after just two. I have always been a bit hyperactive, but my discipline and willpower to work hard have skyrocketed.

Yet, I learned a lot about balance too. I just cancelled a trip to Slovenia. It would be really nice to see my friends and family again. But it would also mean crashing on the couch again and unnecessarily stressful airport runs.

Don't get me wrong, I still travel a lot and love to do it, but I think one or two flights a month are more than enough.

After a full day of hustle I take time to relax, so I don't burn out. I spend some time with a girl I like (yes, Alex is coming to visit me in Barcelona soon too) or just go out and meet some new people. Or go do some breakdance, watch a movie, smoke one.

As I said, I eat really healthy and disciplined, but every now and then, I also eat some crisps or some other unhealthy food. It's like the world tour aged me, not physically, but mentally, in terms of maturity. And I get this from people a lot. They always guess me older.

If I could give any age to Max, I'd say he would be 40. I wouldn't give myself 24. Instead, put Vini and myself at about 30. This age, of course, is a metaphor. But it holds pretty true. We actually act our age. Our experience age that is. And certain things change when you grow older from experience.

You start discarding stuff that's unimportant and start appreciating what is important.

For example, I don't drink that much anymore. And there's nothing wrong with drinking, don't get me wrong. I just don't feel like it, and have no problem letting go without. Plus I hate hangovers. But when I see my friends in their late 30's still getting wasted every weekend, I think to myself that maybe they need to go on a world tour too.

And the moral of this story is, that in order to learn all of this, you need to pay the price.

To be confident and cool with the girls now, I needed to be frustrated in Tallinn. I needed to punch that wall with my fist and release my anger after pulling three times in two days, and not managing to get laid.

To be able to have a beautiful, jaw-dropping hot girl come over, and not be focused only on fucking her, I needed to face a lot of shit from girls, find a lot of flakes, and experience a lot of blue balls.

To be able to shrug it off, if I don't end up getting laid. And to be happy, but not too excited, if I do. To be able to create a beautiful connection that changes lives.

For all that, I needed to get my heart broken over and over again. I needed girls to not text or call me back. I needed to doubt both the game and myself. I needed to be told to fuck off countless times, I needed to screw it all up. And then slowly but surely, a celestial armor of divine confidence emerged. I just increased my hit points exponentially.

To be able to hustle as much as I do now, I needed to work for hours and hours on video editing. I needed to fuck up some projects, and spend hours and days being frustrated on mistakenly deleted files. I needed to work on a project much larger than me, where I thought I'll go mad.

It didn't make me go mad. It just made me stronger.

And to be able to enjoy my stay in a humble room in central Barcelona, I needed to travel around the world for eight months.

Till the next adventure,

Bostjan

Team RSD Max

Signing off.

Chapter Thirty-Three
EPILOGUE – TIME HEALS ALL WOUNDS

London, September 2016

WhatsApp Conversation

Max: *"Sure man, we'll talk about the book and everything else."*

Max: *"By the way, Command & Conquer?"*

Me: *"I dunno bro, having a very long and late travel day."*

Max: *"So… is that a yes? :D :D"*

Me: *"Lol sure, I'll just stand here in the passport check cue, ask someone to hold the computer, another one to hold something for my mouse. And, fuck it, while at it, I'll ask some girl to blow me while we play. Oh, and hopefully, the airport WiFi is good, and we won't get disconnected."*

Max: *"hahaha lelelele, you in London now as far as I remember?"*

Me: *"Yup, yup, just landed. Thursday evening might be C & C friendly, or some afternoon, I'll ping you when I can - you should do the same."*

Max: *"Cool, cool. And dude, I had sex with another hottie yesterday, literally the second stunner I just hooked up with like that."*

Me: *"Omg, Helsinki, fuck my life. Did she have a nice and tight ass? :)))) Knowing you, it's probably more tight than mine, hahahha."*

Max: *"Duuude, and then the blonde girl (the other stunner) that I really love, texts me, how she heard some bad stuff about me. Replied back (late at night) that it's no big deal and most of it is made up.*

Max: *"She then didn't respond cause she was already asleep. Then, in the morning at 6am, she replies telling me that it's okay and that she believes me. Then we hang out again, she shows up in a mini skirt, blonde angel hair, stockings, dude, she's so beautiful man."*

Me: *Wait was it Riika? Or what was that the other blondes name, you told me about her?*

Max: *"She sits next to me paying attention to what I'm saying. Yeah Riika is her name. Then my assistant shows up, we edit, she sits there, not complaining, then I do a live stream while she sits outside of the frame next to me and listens to my rant."*

Max: *"I fucking love this girl so much, haha, awesome social* *proof too, hah. Then my assistant leaves and we fuck on the floor without condom (again). I love this girl so much, man, jesus."*

Max: *"And I'm becoming a good person again, you know, like trusting people and shit."*

Max: *And then we're on a business call: Jim, me, Pete and Johan, she's sitting next to me, pays attention, man I love this girl, dude. Then we watch Jurassic World and just cuddle all day. And she's totally as cuddly as I am, she even slept over the other day."*

Max: *"I couldn't sleep cause I just wanted to hold her in my hands much more than I wanted to sleep. Lel man, and she doesn't care about me being that pua and stuff, she watched some of my videos at home and she just doesn't care."*

Max: *"She's just so easy going man, no drama, no stress and stuff, just such a lovely personality and so fucking hot man. We literally have sex, I come 3 times, then kiss her while I'm still on top of her and i'm getting hard again, man, fuck dude."*

Max: *"You know, you never know how long these honeymoon phases last and you never know many girls can hold back their craziness successfully for a long time, haha but for now man, I just wanna spend all day and all night with her man."*

Me: *"Bro, I think this is fucking amazing, and that you really, really need it.*

Me: *"And how long it lasts...*

Me: *"Fuck it, it's something beautiful, and it will last as long as it will, as long as you two share and enjoy each other, it's all good."*

Max: *"I'm telling you these things cause you're the only person that has such a GOOD personality that you can understand this kind of shit ya know =)"*

Max: *"Yeah man, I literally just lay in bed or sit at my table and think about her and get an instant boner and smile, I wanna travel with her, take her to Istanbul when I get the next tat ;)"*

Me: *"And yeah rly fucking epic man I'm so happy you found this again..."*

Me: *"That's why we started gaming... At least for me!"*

Max: *"Yeah man, that's why I started gaming, dude I swear to god, the first 5 minutes I met her on our first date, all I thought about was "dude, I've never been so happy to actually STAY and live at a place for once."*

Max: *"When we escalated all I said was "hey, let's take this slowly, we'll take our time..." and it felt so good saying it and 100%, no 1000000% meaning it."*

Me: *"Yeah dude, you can only appreciate taking it slow when you are forced to go fast haha, Words of Wisdom lol."*

Me: *"Anyway, my battery is totally dying, hope I find my host trolololo."*

Me: *"But yeah, thanks for sharing this, I really appreciate it."*

Max: *"Haha totally man, ah, man cool no worries, and thanks for listening, I appreciate it as well!"*

Max: *"So thanks bro! I'm just so sad that..."*

Me: *"?"*

Max: *"You still suck at C & C, :) :P :D."*

Me: *"Motherfucker :D Have a good night man, peace!"*

Max: *"Hahaha, save travels mate, talk to you soon!"*

Glossary

The Game
A book by Neill Strauss, and a concept of the male-female
seduction process, the techniques and explanations. You
can have game, or a lack of it. You can do game, you can
game with others, you can game girls, or be gamed, or you
can be a student of the game.

Pimping
Pimping (it) – a slang term which means going out and
talking to women which you didn't know before. Another
term for it is "cold approach pickup". Usually used by
guys in the seduction community.

Wingman
Your friend who helps you get the girl. Either by just
hanging out with you and thus putting you in an awesome
mood, or by actually talking to the girl's friends etc,
allowing you to focus on the girl.

Open
The act of starting the interaction with an unknown
person. Either verbal by saying "Hi", or something else, or
nonverbal, for example by eye-contact, gestures or touch.

Bambi Eyes
When a girl's pupils are very dilated, looking straight into
your eyes, almost without blinking. You can kind of feel
the energy and the "chemistry" as some people would say.

Set
A group of people around the girl you want to talk to. It
can be only 2 people, the girl and a friend, or it can be a big
group.

Inner Circle
A dedicated Facebook group where players meet and discuss different topics. It's a place to find new wingmen, it's a place to ask questions, a place to share ideas and resources. Amazing places, that help the community grow.

Player
A guy (or a girl) who games.

Approach
Same as # Open.

Hook
Hook is a term for a point where a girl is more inclined to stay and talk to you than to leave. She's comfortable being around you for the time, and from there on you can build up on your interaction.

Cocky-Funny
A slang term coined by David D, suggesting a guy be a combination of a funny guy and a dick when he talks to a girl to make her attracted to him. A cocky-funny guy.

Game Fanboy
A dude who watches way too many game videos and who's read way too many books on the topic. Someone who thinks that RSD instructors are basically Gods and eat pussy for breakfast. I used to be one.

Pulling
Going home or another private location with the girl, from the venue your are at currently.

Butt Hurt
A slang term for a guy who's acting like a little bitch. A girl

*doesn't do as he likes, he starts making up drama and blaming her etc. Being Butt Hurt is never good, but happens to the best of us. Another word would be #**Needy**, as in "needing" the girl to do or not do something, and being emotionally dependent on that.*

#Takeaway

When a girl doesn't do what you want her to, you withdraw most of, or all of your attention. Complete emotional withdrawal, it hurts more than fists. And that's why it works. It's highly manipulative, so special care needs to be taken when using this. Or better, don't use it at all.

#Chode

Is a guy who is afraid of being a guy. He's afraid to show that he likes a girl, he thinks liking sex is bad, he feels bad about expressing what he really feels and wants. A lot of this is to blame on the whole society's instruction of what a cool guy should be but not all of it. We also call chode pretty much any guy who does not know about the game.

#Close

Close is an end-point stage in interaction between a guy and a girl. There's different closes, for example the number-close, or #close, kiss-close. There's the old school slang term f-close, which means a fuck-close. You also have a Facebook-close or basically anything you can think of.

#In/Out Of State

When you're in state, you feel amazing. You had it in your life before too, it can happen in sports, your job, at a game. It's when everything seems to click, it's when you open girls and they all hook. It's when you get make outs just like that. It's when you have zero fear and feel invincible. How to get that? Usually it's a process of talking to so many girls that you don't care anymore. You let go of your fears and restrictions and just become truly genuine and in the moment. But there's random factors too. It's quite hard to explain.

#Isolate
When you move a girl to the bar or some other area of the club where you two can have a conversation. For example, if she's around her friends, it's a lot less likely she'll be okay with you two kissing, because all the friends might judge her. If you guys are alone, that's not an issue.

#Seed the Pull
When you start making future plans for the night with the girl. Either mentioning the two of you might get some food later on, or check out a movie, or get a drink, or have a walk. Basically, anything that signals you want to spend more time with her. So when the clubs closes, or when you make a move, she kinda knows, she's not surprised.

#Self-Amusement
A principle in game. You should never be dependent on how you feel internally on external stimulii, meaning your friends, alcohol, music or some girl's approval. You should find this in yourself. To make it less deep, an example is you talking about Borat jokes in the club, even though the other speaker might not consider them funny. But you do, and that's what matters.If they don't like that they are free to leave, and you can find someone who will enjoy jokes like that.

#Screen Logistics
Get information on where the girl lives, how many friends is she in the club with, and what is she doing the day after. All important factors to consider, when deciding to invite the girl to your/her place or not.

#Flake

When a girl doesn't respond to your texts or calls, or doesn't show up at a date.

#Anti-Slut Defense

When a girl is sexually interested with you, but does not want to take things further, because she is concerned with how she might look to others. Example, if she just goes home with a guy after an hour, even though there's awesome connection or just pure attraction, she would feel guilty and considered a "slut" in eyes of others. Also called connected to #Slut-Shaming

#Down-To-Fuck (DTF)

How much a girl is in a state of mind to have sex that night.

#White Knight

A guy who sees the typical maiden in distress and believes that he can help her. He sees the girl as the pure innocent goddess, who cannot help or save herself. Here his chivalry and virtue shine, and he charges to the rescue.

#Reference Experience

In game, we count every single interaction, whether good or bad as a reference experience. It's quite simple, as long as you reflect, every single reference experience, regardless of result, will make your game better.

#Door Game

When the club is closing or about to close. You leave the club and linger around close to the front door. When girl come out, you just chat them up, screening if they might be down for an after party or food. Surprisingly, you can pull from there.

Instant Date

Usually happens when day gaming. After screening the girls and seeing that they have some time on their hands, you can instantly take them to a coffee shop, to the park, or whenever you want to go. Since you just met them a few minutes ago, this is called an instant date.

Acknowledgements

This is, quite egoistically, one of my favorite parts of the book. I like being grateful, and there are a lot of people to be grateful to in the process of putting out this book.

First of all, to the heroes of the book, Max and Vini, for accepting me on the road with them for so long, and for keeping me company on the biggest adventure of my life (so far). Without them, not one of these words on the page would have come to be.

To all the amazing women I've meet on the travels in Vienna, Oslo, Berlin, Sofia, Bucharest, Krakow, London, Helsinki, Tallinn. I will not forget you ladies, our times together, and my lessons. I hope I get to see some of you again.

To all the early readers of this book. It would never ever become this good without you, thank you!

To all the hosts that offered me their couch, room, bed, or floor. I am deeply grateful. When I have enough money to rent a nice apartment for myself, I will always keep an extra room, and invite people from all over the world to crash there for free. I promise.

To my bros, Ward and Benjamin, that have my back when I need it. And to Ward, additionally, for making me apply for the job in the first place.

To my family, for supporting what I do.

To Alex, for showing me what love is.

To Fernando from ClickDo, to push me into becoming a personal brand, and for financial support along the way. I would not have made it without you.

To my brother Simon, for the help and support in the whole process. And even more importantly, to teach my one of the most important truths ever - that Google knows everything.

To my stupid boss, who let me quit my job as a therapeutic youth worker a few months prior to the tour. I'd never experience this bitter sweet adventure without her being so dumb.

To the community. For the years of support in the form of random comments, likes, field reports and advice. Both on and off-line. For motivation to persist and improve. I wouldn't have made it solo.

Author Bio

Bostjan has always liked reading. As a 9 year old child he read Lord of the Rings three times, both in Slovenian and English. He was familiar with most of the books on the shelf at the local library.

However, as testosterone took its course, the avid reader started to focus much more of his attention on women and sports than reading. So instead of reading, he'd prefer to breakdance, go out and drink, and think about how cool it would be to actually get laid.

In the early adult years, he started to move around the world a lot. That included an exchange year in Lithuania, a year of working with aggressive kids in London, and then finally traveling the world with an elite dating coach.

The love of reading somehow emerged back to the surface in the form of writing, and the result is the book you have in front of you right now.

If you have any questions or would like to say hello, don't hesitate to contact him via email at bostjan.belingar@gmail.com, or engage him on his social media or blog.

Further Resources

If you're inspired and interested after reading about these adventures, here's a few ideas on what to do next:

1) Follow Bostjan on **www.bosslifehacks.com**. There's a lot of advice, stories, and epiphanies touching on various subjects. It's a sort of playground where everything is allowed. You will also find **Bosslifehacks** on Youtube and Instagram.

Make sure to put in your email address/subscribe there - I'll shoot you a value-giving email once or twice a month. No spamming, I promise.

2) Make me a favor:

If you liked this book, please drop a review on Amazon. This is one of the main factors that influences people's buying decisions. So if you take a minute to drop a review (it can be super short), I will be eternally grateful. Plus you increase your karma +5.

No really, please do that :)

3) If you're interested in seduction, game, and players, there's a lot you can do. If you want to learn the techniques yourself, check out an ultimate course called The Natural on basically everything you need to know from my good friend and the hero of this book, RSD Max. And if you are struggling with fear, jump on board of the FEARLESS crew, and demolish it forever.

Made in the USA
Middletown, DE
27 August 2017